353.03 Fincher, Ernest B.
FIN
    The presidency

| DATE | | | |
|---|---|---|---|
| MAY 23 '85 | | | |
| MAY 11 '88 | | | |
| AP 20 '95 | | | |
| | | | |
| | | | |
| | | | |
| | | | |
| | | | |
| | | | |
| | | | |
| | | | |

# THE
# PRESIDENCY

## AN AMERICAN
## INVENTION

# THE
# PRESIDENCY

# AN AMERICAN
# INVENTION

by

# ERNEST B. FINCHER

Abelard-Schuman
New York

Library of Congress Cataloging in Publication Data  Fincher, Ernest Barksdale, The Presidency: An American Invention  Bibliography: p. Includes index. SUMMARY: *Examines the office and powers of the Presidency citing specific actions, decisions, and ideas of different Presidents.* 1. Presidents—United States—Juv. lit. [1. Presidents] I. Title. JK517.F55    353.03'13    77-103    ISBN 0-200-00177-9

1  2  3  4  5  6  7  8  9  10

TO MY SISTERS
DOROTHY CURRIE AND LOUISE STELL

# PREFACE

THE PRESIDENCY: AN AMERICAN INVENTION is a new approach
to the office of Chief Executive. The textbook organization,
with its stress on mechanics, has been rejected in favor of
what may be described as a layman's view of the most important elective office in the Western World. The goal has
been a succinctly written book that will hold the reader's
interest, while providing him with a great fund of information. The office and powers of the Presidency are fully
treated, and the principles involved are set forth by actual
example. Dramatic episodes are freely employed, not only
to make the rights and the responsibilities of the President
more real, but also to illuminate the character of the Chief
Executive.

Readers should find the Appendix very helpful in gaining
a better understanding of the Presidency. Besides the sec-

tions of the Constitution that pertain to the Presidency, the Appendices provide a great deal of biographical data on the Presidents and Vice-Presidents, along with a select reading list that is classified according to subject matter.

A work of this nature is of necessity a cooperative enterprise. Thus many people have given direct and indirect assistance in the preparation of THE PRESIDENCY. Particular gratitude should be expressed to Harry Balfe and Gilbert O. Hourtoule, professors of political science at the New Jersey State College at Montclair, for their very helpful criticism of the manuscript. I am also indebted to Robert R. Parsons, formerly of Teachers College, Columbia University, who read the manuscript with matters of format and style in mind, and to Morrell Gipson, my editor at Abelard-Schuman. A number of librarians have been helpful in providing material for this book. Special mention must be made of the curators of the picture collections of the New York Public Library, the Library of Congress, and the New-York Historical Society. Various publishers and government agencies have been kind enough to permit the use of pictures and charts. These have been individually acknowledged with the customary credit lines.

It goes without saying that for the statement of fact and the interpretation of events the responsibility is altogether mine.

ERNEST B. FINCHER

# CONTENTS

ix

# CONTENTS

# I

# THE PRESIDENT: FIRST AMONG EQUALS

The crowd cheered as men and boys pushed the barge from the wharf. Then the crew dipped oars in precision, and the craft moved majestically across the bay. The people left behind could easily follow the progress of the barge because it was painted red, white, and blue, and the members of its crew were dressed in white. Onlookers could even count the oarsmen: there were thirteen of them, one for each state in the Union. The number had been chosen as a tribute both to the chief passenger on the barge and to the occasion for his journey. . . . George Washington was being conveyed from the New Jersey shore to New York City for his inauguration as the first President of the United States of America.

Hundreds of boats, all of them decked with flags, fell in behind the barge, and as the fleet neared the Staten Island battery, cannons boomed. A Spanish warship anchored in the harbor answered the salute with a deafening cannonade of its own. Then porpoises began to play around the barge that carried the first President. It was considered a good omen.

There seemed every reason for George Washington to be content. His journey from Mount Vernon had been a triumphant procession. His coach had been escorted first by one troop of cavalry and then another. Throngs of people had cheered him from both sides of the road, and the leading citizens of each town he passed through had feted him with a banquet, a reception, or a display of fireworks. Now as his barge crossed the bay, he was surrounded by his adoring countrymen. He knew that once he set foot on land, thousands of his fellow citizens would receive him with undisguised affection and respect.

That knowledge filled him with misgiving. He had not wanted to be the first President of the republic that he had helped to form. In fact, he had accepted the office only because he had been persuaded that to do so was his duty. His close friend James Madison, "the Father of the Constitution," had summarized the universal feeling when he assured the general that he was the only feature of the new government that had really captured the imagination of the people. At one time, the fate of the young republic had rested in the hands of George Washington, Commander of the Continental Army. Now the fate of the republic was in the hands of George Washington, President-elect of the United States. Madison, Hamilton, and the other Founding Fathers believed that the form the government took—in fact, its very survival—depended upon Washington's conduct of the presidential office, which was the keystone of the system. The thought was sobering. What lay ahead promised to be no easier to endure than the woes that had beset him during seven grim years of war.

The welcoming crowd in New York City was even larger than Washington had expected, and the arrangements for his reception were even more elaborate. The governor of the state received him and escorted him to the coach that was waiting to take him to the mansion set aside for his use. After that, there was a great banquet, with members of Congress and other notables in attendance.

The festivities that marked Washington's arrival in New York, the first capital of the United States, were impressive, but the inauguration itself was even more brilliantly executed. On April 30, 1789, he awakened to the sound of the thirteen guns that were being fired from the battery on Manhattan Island. The President-to-be dressed in an American-made broadcloth suit, and a valet powdered his hair. Church bells began to ring, as if summoning everyone in the city to say a prayer for the new government. Crowds gathered outside the presidential mansion hours before the inaugural procession was to form. At last a coach drawn by four prancing horses drew up at the door. Washington was driven to Federal Hall, an imposing building that had been remodeled as the seat of the new republic. Members of Congress received Washington at the entrance and escorted him to the balcony above. There he could see the thousands of his countrymen who had gathered in the streets, at windows, and on rooftops to watch his inauguration as their first President.

The chief justice of New York State administered the oath

THE FIRST INAUGURATION.   Washington's inauguration on April 30, 1789, marked the beginning of a great experiment in government. The launching of the United States of America was regarded even at that time as an important milestone in the development of democracy. *(Courtesy of The New York-Historical Society, New York City)*

4

of office, and then turned to the waiting crowd and shouted, "Long live George Washington, President of the United States!" The throng responded with a prolonged cheer. When Washington bowed, the shouts became even louder. As the President left the balcony to deliver his inaugural address to the waiting Congress, the crowd watched the Stars and Stripes being raised over the seat of government. The guns of the battery saluted the rising flag with a deafening round of shot.

## EARLY CONCEPTS OF THE PRESIDENCY

In the weeks that followed his inauguration, Washington had many occasions to consider the nature of the office that he occupied. No one was better qualified to interpret the constitutional provisions that related to the Presidency. By unanimous vote, the delegates to the Constitutional Convention had made Washington their presiding officer. In that role he had heard and considered every view exposed in the course of debate. Moreover, ideas that he refrained from offering in public during the extended discussion, he had felt free to express in private, particularly to those members of the convention whose arguments carried weight.

No feature of the new Constitution had caused more discussion than the executive branch of government. Most of the delegates agreed that the federal government should have three distinct branches—legislative, executive, and judicial—and that the powers given to each should be held in check and balanced by the authority granted the other two. The delegates had not found it particularly difficult to agree on the general character of the Congress and the authority

5

that it was to exercise. But when it came to the nature of the executive branch of government, there was a wide difference of opinion.

Some delegates had come to Philadelphia with the idea that a constitutional monarchy was the ideal form of government. In that system, a king rules in accordance with a fundamental law or charter, and his power is offset by that of a strong legislature and judiciary. Records show that several delegates had thought of a son of George III or a young German prince as a possible first king of the United States. But even though various delegates to the Constitutional Convention may have entertained the idea of establishing a monarchy, the project never became the subject of debate. One thing was certain: the proposal would not be acceptable to the general public, which held monarchs in low regard.

As a matter of fact, some members of the convention had become so suspicious of kings and royal governors that they wanted the executive authority of the new government entrusted to three men, not one. These delegates reasoned that three executives would check one another and thus prevent the growth of tyranny. But after considerable debate, the advocates of a plural—rather than a single—executive were overruled. Having agreed on an executive branch headed by a President, the delegates differed as to how he should be chosen. Some wanted the President to be elected directly by the people of the United States. The advocates of this system argued that direct election was the most democratic way of choosing the Chief Executive, and that voters could be trusted to select an able person as their leader. (Some historians say that the advocates of direct election were confident that George Washington could be induced to offer himself as a candidate. Washington would be the overwhelming choice of voters, who would keep him in office as long as he lived.)

But a majority of the convention delegates were unwilling to allow such an important official to be elected by the people as a whole. Some members believed that ordinary citizens would not be capable of making a proper choice. Others mistrusted the common people, and did not want to place too much authority in their hands. For those reasons, opponents of popular election argued that the President should be elected by state legislatures, by the governors of all the states, or by the Congress of the United States. The first two proposals were soon rejected. To choose the President by either means would give the state governments too much control over the federal union, besides encouraging the development of a privileged class of officeholders. At length, the convention decided to have Congress elect the President.

But a number of delegates were unhappy with the arrangement. They reasoned that if the legislative branch chose the Chief Executive, then the President would be subject to the will of Congress. If the delegates were intent upon having three coequal branches of government that checked and balanced one another, then the President must be elected independently of the Congress.

In the last days of the convention, a compromise was reached. Election of the President by Congress was finally rejected in favor of a unique system worked out by a committee. Each state would choose presidential electors equal to the number of its senators and representatives. These electors would meet in the capitals of their states on a day set

7

by Congress. Each elector would have two votes to cast for the candidate whom he regarded as most worthy of being the President of the United States. The results from each state would be forwarded to the national capital, where Congress would count the ballots. The candidate receiving the greatest number of electoral votes would become President; the candidate receiving the second highest number would be the Vice-President. (In the election of 1800, Thomas Jefferson and Aaron Burr received the same number of electoral votes. In accordance with rules laid down by the Constitution, the House of Representatives broke the tie in favor of Jefferson. Not long afterward, the Constitution was amended so that each elector cast one vote for President and one for Vice-President.)

Once the delegates agreed upon a method of electing the President, the general character of the executive branch of government took final form. In establishing the office of President of the United States, the Founding Fathers created a unique kind of ruler. The Presidency was unlike any other office then in existence. As one observer put it, the Constitutional Convention hit upon the idea of an elective king. Executive power was placed in the hands of one person, elected outside the legislature. But unlike a hereditary monarch, the President had a fixed term of office, even though he might be reelected. Moreover he could be removed by Congress for certain offenses that were defined in the Constitution.

To protect executive independence, the President was granted major powers of his own in Article II of the Constitution. In other words, his authority was to come from the very source of government, rather than from grants by

THE FIRST PRESIDENT AND THE THIRTY-NINTH PRESI-
DENT. George Washington was inaugurated almost two hundred years
ago, but the stamp he placed upon the Presidency is still apparent. The
thirty-ninth President, Jimmy Carter, acknowledged the fact by holding a
press conference under the portrait of the first President in the Capitol
building, Washington, D.C., shortly after his election. (*Wide World Photos*)

Congress. To put it briefly, the framers of the Constitution created in the President of the United States of America a far more independent, a far more powerful official than anyone had thought possible when the delegates first assembled in Philadelphia. Clinton Rossiter, a leading authority on American government, summed up the will of the Convention when he wrote that the "President was to be a strong, dignified, nonpolitical chief of state and government. In two words, he was to be George Washington."

## THE NEW OFFICE TAKES FORM

Washington was elected President by the unanimous vote of the Electoral College—the only President who has ever received such an honor. As the hero of the American people, he bestowed great prestige on the office that he so reluctantly assumed. And yet he was aware that the Presidency was feared by many of his countrymen, among them men whom he greatly respected. These critics were afraid that the President of the United States was dangerously akin to a monarch. They believed that once in office, a President might very well gain control of the government and rule like a king, even though he might not have the title.

On the other hand, some of Washington's friends believed that the United States was floundering, and that what it needed was the firm direction that only a strong executive could provide. In appearance, Washington was more regal than most kings. Then let him rule like one, but always subject to the restraints imposed by the Constitution.

So as Washington assumed office, he was all too aware that

one faction of his fellow countrymen believed that the government he represented was likely to become an agent of oppression. The other faction was afraid that he would shrink from using the vast authority that the Constitution conferred on him.

The problem was to exalt the new government without threatening the rights of the people of the United States, and to make the Presidency a highly effective office without damaging democratic institutions. It was a hard policy to pursue. The first President was aware that he would be establishing precedents that would be followed as long as the United States of America endured.

The skillful manner in which Washington gave form to the Presidency was demonstrated in many ways. At the very outset of his administration, he developed a line of conduct that he proposed to follow. He believed that the people of the United States expected their leader to represent in his person the pride and dignity of a rising nation. They wanted the President of their republic to merit the respect that Europeans showed their kings. Accordingly the first President became a master showman, either consciously or from design. Many years later, John Adams, the second President, acknowledged Washington's success in creating an image of the way the Chief Executive should look and act. Adams said that Washington "understood this Art very well, and we may say of him, if he was not the greatest President, he was the best Actor of the Presidency we ever had."

Physically Washington was imposing. He was a head taller than most of his countrymen, and he had a majestic bearing. He enhanced an already impressive appearance by dressing handsomely. He always rode the finest horse that money could buy, seated in a silver-fitted saddle that had a leopard skin showing underneath it. The great coach that he used on state occasions was drawn by six cream-colored horses matched for size. Liveried servants were in attendance, and outriders in uniform rode alongside the President.

Although deeply involved in political affairs, Washington did not neglect the social aspects of the Presidency. In fact, with the aid of his wife he made social gatherings a highly important feature of his administration. Martha Washington, a noteworthy person in her own right, did not reach New York until after the inauguration. Her arrival from Mount Vernon in a resplendent coach heightened interest in the position that her husband occupied. Although criticized because she entertained lavishly and in a very formal manner, Martha Washington became the acknowledged leader of society, and citizens in all parts of the nation were impressed by the grand yet friendly manner in which she fulfilled her duties as the President's wife. From her time onward, the First Ladies of the United States have exerted influence, sometimes as social leaders, sometimes as their husbands' counselors, sometimes as champions of the underprivileged and despised.

Some Americans ridiculed the Washington "court," as they described it. But his defenders called attention to the staunchly democratic character of Washington's conduct of government. It fulfilled the hopes of Americans who wanted a strong executive, yet quieted the minds of most of those who had feared that the President might take as his model the repressive kings of Europe.

Washington, for example, did not seek to rule alone, but shared the decision-making power with his associates. He

**SOCIAL ASPECTS OF THE PRESIDENCY.** Martha Washington used social functions to create support for the government that her husband directed. The ball that concludes Inauguration Day is the beginning of a round of dinners, receptions, concerts, and other social activities that continue during a President's tenure of office. Depicted here is the ball held to honor William McKinley after his inaugural in 1897. *(From* Harper's Weekly, *courtesy of the Library of Congress)*

13

surrounded himself with advisers of distinction, and in making his appointments, he was careful to choose citizens from all parts of the nation—a precedent that Presidents have followed to this day. Hamilton, Jefferson, Knox, and Randolph were named as heads of the executive departments, and they set in motion the machinery of the federal government. Washington established another precedent when he brought together for consultation his attorney general and his secretaries of state, war, and treasury. From these early meetings, the presidential cabinet developed—a feature of government not mentioned in the Constitution but one that soon became an integral part of the American political system.

In his dealings with Congress, President Washington recognized the limitations that the Constitution placed on his own power. The Congress of the United States was given authority to make policy in the form of legislation. It was the President's duty to execute the law. But the first President would not allow the legislative branch to infringe upon the authority that the Constitution granted the Chief Executive. For example, when the House of Representatives demanded the right to examine correspondence relating to a treaty with Great Britain, Washington refused on the grounds that the Constitution gave the President the sole right to conduct foreign relations. He reinforced the point by successfully claiming the right to recognize in the name of the United States the independence of a new nation or a change of government in an established nation. When Washington issued a proclamation stating that the United States would be neutral in the war between England and France, he angered many members of Congress and other leading

Americans. But Washington's neutrality proclamation established yet another precedent for future Presidents to follow.

In the conduct of domestic affairs, the first President also gave form to the executive office. A noteworthy example was the manner in which he reacted to the Pennsylvania frontiersmen who challenged the right of federal revenue officers to collect taxes on home-distilled whisky. Washington took a serious view of the dispute, which he considered defiance of the national government. As President, he was commander in chief of the armed forces of the United States. Utilizing that power, he ordered the mobilization of an army larger than any he had commanded during the Revolutionary War. He set out for western Pennsylvania at the head of this imposing force, but the "Whisky Rebellion" collapsed before the federal army reached the troubled area.

The President's prompt response to what he regarded as a challenge to federal authority made a profound impression, and it magnified the role of the national government in the eyes of the American people. A much less dramatic but equally important act occurred during Washington's first nationwide tour. To cement the hold of the new government on the lives of the American people, the first President undertook two ambitious and exhausting tours, one through New England and another through the South. When Washington reached Boston, a social crisis that had important political overtones developed. John Hancock, the governor of Massachusetts, decided that the President should call on him since he was the chief executive of the host state, which was one of the most important in the nation. Washington believed that the governor of Massachusetts should first call on the President, who represented the people of all the states. For two days, both the President and the governor refused to yield. Then Governor Hancock swallowed his pride and paid tribute to federal authority by calling on the President at his headquarters. By his insistence, Washington underlined the fact that the federal government was superior to the states in certain areas defined by the Constitution.

## TO BE GREAT IS TO BE MISUNDERSTOOD

Washington came to office as a national hero. As President, his dedication, political skill, and firm leadership strengthened not only the executive branch but also the entire national government. But neither his own stature nor his position as President of the United States protected Washington from attack. For while the vast majority continued to venerate their chosen leader, he had a number of savage critics. They fell upon him from all quarters, but principally in newspapers, pamphlets, and cartoons. Washington's enemies charged that he acted like a king and wanted to be one, and that in strengthening the federal government he endangered the states and threatened to destroy the liberty of the people.

The unfairness of the charges wounded a proud man who had made many sacrifices for his country. In public, the President maintained a dignified silence, however vicious the attack. In private, he sometimes raged. One of Washington's associates reported that after the fury played out, the President sank exhausted in despondency. What Washington learned so painfully, every President who followed him was to find out: the more positive the executive leadership, the more violent the criticism in Congress and the press.

Washington had accepted the Presidency with great reluctance. As the end of his first term of office approached, he longed to be rid of the thankless role that had been thrust upon him, and to return to his beloved Mount Vernon. Hints that Washington's first term would be his last filled many statesmen with alarm. They regarded Washington's continuance in office as essential to the survival of the republic. The reasons for this belief were plain to see. The United States was in danger of being drawn into the war that raged in Europe. The British had not surrendered the western territory, as they were required to do by the treaty that ended the Revolution. Political factions had developed within the nation, and partisan strife threatened to destroy the newly created federal government.

It was generally believed that only Washington could lead the nation through the dangers that beset it. While Thomas Jefferson no longer supported many of Washington's policies, he recognized the necessity of keeping the first President in office. And so he wrote that Washington was "the only man in the United States who possessed the confidence of the whole. . . . and that the longer he remained, the stronger would become the habits of the people in submitting to the Government, and in thinking it a thing to be maintained; that there was no other person who would be thought anything more than the head of a party." Jefferson assured Washington himself that "your being at the helm will be more than an answer to every argument which can be used to alarm and lead the people in any quarter into violence or secession. North and South will hang together if they have you to hang on."

Washington allowed himself to be persuaded that it was his duty to accept a second term of office. And having been elected again by unanimous vote of the Electoral College, he continued to exercise authority with understanding and restraint. But he made it clear that two terms of office were all that he would consent to serve, thus making it necessary for political leaders to consider who would be his successor. In refusing to serve for more than two terms, Washington established a precedent that proved binding for almost 150 years, and that was broken only because the nation was becoming involved in a war that threatened its existence. (Franklin D. Roosevelt, whose term of office extended from 1933 to 1945, was the only President who ever served more than two terms.)

Washington gave form to the Presidency until the day he left office. And in his Farewell Address to the American people he placed his stamp on future domestic and foreign policy. He first admonished his countrymen to avoid partisan strife, because division would weaken the nation. He then made his famous remarks on foreign policy, words of advice that guided future Presidents. The retiring Chief Executive cautioned that the United States was still a weak nation in a world dominated by the powerful monarchies of Europe. But the new republic had the distinct advantage of being removed from the scene of conflict by a vast expanse of ocean. Thus protected, the United States should pursue its commercial interests, and make itself strong enough to resist attack. Above all, the young nation should avoid being drawn into European wars. To this end, Washington concluded, the United States should avoid entangling alliances with other nations.

Having given parting advice that if followed would protect the nation that he had done so much to form, Washington retired to Mount Vernon, intending to pursue the life of a country gentleman. But having left the Presidency, he became an elder statesman whose advice was often sought, particularly when a crisis developed in the government. And much of his time and thought was given to the development of a permanent capital for his country, a city so well planned and so handsomely built that it would be a credit to the nation. The city that bears his name is a monument to the first President of the United States. In the opinion of some of his biographers, the Presidency itself is also something of a monument to the first Chief Executive. He took a new and unformed institution and developed it into an office of formidable power, but an office subject to the popular will. He proved that presidential powers could be used to advance the interests of the people as a whole, rather than the people of one class or one section of the country. In accomplishing that much, Washington placed his stamp on the Presidency, and helped to make the office a distinct contribution to the political systems of the world.

# II

# THE LURE
# OF THE
# PRESIDENCY

In the year that Washington became President, the French people revolted against their royal government and subsequently beheaded their king and queen. News of the French Revolution sent a wave of excitement across the United States. Americans gratefully remembered that French military support had enabled them to win their independence. Moreover, democratic principles set forth by a number of French writers had greatly influenced the Founding Fathers, thus helping to determine the character of American government. And so when European monarchs threatened to destroy the newly established French Republic, thousands of Americans insisted that their government should support France.

But President Washington opposed American interference

in European affairs. He believed that if the United States were drawn into war, the nation would be gravely injured, if not ruined. For that reason, he resisted all efforts to have the United States join the side of the French people. Washington's policy of neutrality angered a large part of the populace, who insisted that their country was honor bound not only to repay the debt it owed France but also to support a fellow democracy.

Despite the great prestige that George Washington enjoyed, many Americans wanted him removed from office because he insisted on neutrality. Philadelphia, where the capital had been removed from New York, was a stronghold of pro-French sentiment. Day after day the streets of the capital were filled with angry crowds. According to John Adams, the Vice-President, "Ten thousand people . . . threatened to drag Washington out of his house and effect a revolution in the government." Adams maintained that the President escaped being overturned only because an epidemic of yellow fever struck Philadelphia. As victims of the disease began to die in great numbers, panic developed, and thousands of people fled the city. Political matters were forgotten.

The threat to Washington's life was an early reminder that Presidents live dangerously. In that instance, a mob seemed ready to take the life of an almost universally revered leader. But later Presidents were threatened by individual assassins, and several were struck down by their assailants. In 1835, Andrew Jackson escaped assassination at the hands of a mentally unbalanced man only because both pistols used by the would-be assassin misfired. The next three attempts on a President's life were successful. Abraham Lincoln (1865),

James Garfield (1881), and William McKinley (1901) were all assassinated while in office.

As former President Theodore Roosevelt was campaigning for another term of office in 1912, he narrowly escaped assassination. The bullet intended for him was deflected by a metal case that held his glasses and by the thick folds of paper that the candidate had put into his breast pocket after making last-minute changes in the speech he was about to make. In 1933, Franklin D. Roosevelt, the President-elect of the United States, was the intended victim of a deranged man. The bullets meant for the future President killed the mayor of Chicago, who was in Roosevelt's party, and wounded four other persons. While the White House was being remodeled in 1950, President Truman and his family lived in Blair House, which is across the street from the Executive Mansion. The President's temporary residence was attacked by two men who had been active in the Puerto Rican independence movement. The assassins killed a presidential guard before one of them was wounded fatally and the other was captured. President John F. Kennedy was assassinated in 1963. In 1975, two attempts were made on the life of President Ford, in each instance while he was campaigning in California.

This brief account of assassinations and attempted assassinations makes it clear that the President leads a very dangerous life. And yet no person in the world is more closely guarded. The Secret Service, which is charged with protecting the President and certain other public officials, has some three thousand agents, many of whom accompany the President wherever he goes. Other agents make elaborate preparations for domestic and foreign travel, while the greater part of the service is involved in the day-by-day protection of the President while he is in Washington.

When the President travels by land, he ordinarily rides in a bulletproof limousine, accompanied by hundreds of federal, state, and local security officers. His route has already been surveyed; possible assailants have been removed from the scene by detaining persons known to be hostile or mentally unbalanced; and all the food served the presidential party is prepared under security supervision.

When the President travels by air, he flies in a heavily guarded plane that is escorted by military craft. The crew is specially chosen; the route has been scouted; every possible emergency has been foreseen and guarded against. And on the President's trips abroad, even more stringent security measures are in force. Thus when President Nixon made his historic trips to the People's Republic of China and to the Soviet Union in the early 1970s, the American leader traveled under the protection of both his own security forces and those of the nation he was visiting.

Despite the elaborate precautions taken to safeguard the Chief Executive, whenever he moves about, his life is in danger. Yet every President of the United States has insisted on meeting the people of the nation face to face. President Jimmy Carter, for example, walked at the head of his inaugural parade, despite the misgivings of the Secret Service agents who were responsible for his protection.

Even a President whose life has been threatened regards it as his privilege and his duty to mingle with the crowds that surround him wherever he goes. This custom, which dates from the time of George Washington, makes the President vulnerable to attack, either by some mentally ill person or by someone politically motivated. Even candidates for the presidential nomination of their party lead perilous lives. Governor George Wallace of Alabama, for example, was attacked while he was campaigning for the Democratic presidential nomination in 1972. The victim was partially paralyzed by the would-be assassin's bullet, a tragedy that caused the Secret Service to tighten its protection of presidential candidates.

It is not only that the President frequently risks assassination. His daily routine is exhausting because of the heavy demands made upon him. Only a short time before he became a presidential candidate, Woodrow Wilson described the grim life of the Chief Executive. "I don't want to be President," he said. "It's an awful thing to be President of the United States. . . . It means giving up nearly everything that one holds dear." He then explained that when anyone becomes President, he loses all hope of a normal life. In Wilson's opinion, the Presidency acts as a barrier between a man and his family. He becomes a slave to his job. No longer is he able to speak or to act with complete freedom.

## "THE PRESIDENTIAL DISEASE"

If the Presidency is a dangerous, rigorous, thankless job, why do so many Americans covet the office? Why did Wilson, after describing the presidential office in such dismal language, work hard to be nominated?

According to James Reston of *The New York Times*, one of the great mysteries of human life is why intelligent men become so addicted to seeking the Presidency that they cannot rid themselves of the habit, even after years of strenuous, futile effort. The answer to Reston's question may be found in a typically picturesque remark of President Theodore Roosevelt. The ambition to be President is a disease, Roosevelt said, and once "the presidential bug gets into your blood, nothing can remove it except embalming fluid."

At first glance, the financial and social aspects of the Presidency may appear to be its chief attractions. The President's annual salary is $200,000, and that figure is enhanced by an expense allowance of $50,000 and a travel allowance of $40,000. When the President leaves office, he receives an annual pension of $60,000 for life, plus a liberal allowance for maintaining a staff of assistants. And as former President, the retired Chief Executive can count on a handsome income from his published memoirs of office. (President Grant, for example, was paid $500,000 for an account of his life, and some later Presidents have received far larger sums for their memoirs.)

To the average citizen, the President seems to be generously paid. Moreover, his salary and allowances represent only a small part of the benefits of office. He lives more royally than the kings of bygone ages. In fact, *U.S. News and World Report* recently estimated that a private citizen would need an annual income of approximately $35 million to live on the same level as the President of the United States. His official residence is a mansion with 132 rooms, set in an eighteen-acre park in the heart of Washington. To maintain the White House, the President has an annual budget in excess of $3 million. From the White House lawn, he travels to Camp David, his weekend retreat, by helicopter. The "camp" is actually a lavish country estate, replete with golf course, swimming pool, bowling alleys, shooting range, and bad-

SOUTH EXECUTIVE AVE.

1600 PENNSYLVANIA AVENUE, WASHINGTON, D.C. The White House is the most famous residence in the United States, and the goal of countless ambitious Americans. This view of the Executive Mansion and its

A — *American Elm*
JOHN Q. ADAMS

B — *Magnolia Grandiflora*
ANDREW JACKSON

C — *Scarlet Oaks*
BENJAMIN HARRISON

D — *Japanese Maples*
GROVER CLEVELAND

E — *Pin Oak*
WILLIAM McKINLEY

F — *American Elm*
WOODROW WILSON

# KEY

G — *Magnolia Grandiflora*
WARREN G. HARDING

H — *European White Birch*
CALVIN COOLIDGE

I — *American Elm*
J — *White Oak*
HERBERT HOOVER

K — *Magnolia Grandiflora*
L — *White Oak*
M — *Little-leaf Lindens*
FRANKLIN D. ROOSEVELT

N — *American Boxwood*
HARRY S TRUMAN

O — *Black Walnut*
P — *Pin Oak*     Q — *Red Oak*
R — *Northern Red Oak*
DWIGHT D. EISENHOWER

surrounding grounds emphasizes notable trees and the Presidents who had them planted. (*Copyright by White House Historical Association, photograph by National Geographic Society*) minton court. At the President's command is a fleet of auto-mobiles driven by chauffeurs, and a 92-foot yacht and a 60-foot cruiser operated by the navy. The President flies in the flagship of what has been called the world's most exclusive airline—a fleet of twenty-nine planes of advanced design. His own plane, Air Force 1, has luxurious living quarters, an office, and a communications center that keeps the Chief Executive in touch with all parts of the world.

The President is waited upon by a large staff of servants and cared for by his personal physician. First-run movies are always available in the White House projection room; bands and orchestras from the armed forces are available for social functions. Stars of television, stage, and screen vie for the honor of performing in the Executive Mansion.

Lavish though the presidential living standard may be, it is not the chief reason why so many Americans want to occupy the White House. Many successful lawyers and corporation executives are paid far higher salaries than the President receives, and they also live luxuriously. The heads of important universities and foundations are generously paid, enjoy great prestige, and may hold office for decades, while the President may not serve more than two four-year terms.

In seeking to explain why so many Americans aspire to be President, factors other than the ones so far mentioned must be considered. One very obvious attraction of the Presidency is the fact that the Chief Executive always occupies the center of the national stage. No television or motion-picture star, and no hero of the world of sports, can vie with the President in holding the attention of the American people. Whether idolized, distrusted, or disliked, the President of the

THE POWER OF THE PRESIDENT. The awesome authority wielded by
the President of the United States is symbolized by this photograph of
President Franklin D. Roosevelt, flanked by his secretary of the navy and his
ambassador to Mexico, as he reviewed the fleet in New York Harbor, 1934.
*(Naval History Photograph)*

29

United States is its number-one figure. The spotlight follows him wherever he goes. This distinction was remarked as soon as Washington assumed office. The first President enhanced the prestige of his office and strengthened his hold on the hearts of his countrymen by his carefully staged national tours. President Monroe traveled even more extensively, much to his satisfaction and that of the general public. All other public figures were thrown into eclipse by the splendor shed by a President on parade.

After Andrew Jackson took office, he received even greater adulation than his predecessors. When he traveled, the crowds that he attracted were vast for that day. On one of his trips, thirty thousand people greeted him when his ship put in at the Philadelphia navy yard. More than a hundred thousand people turned out for his arrival in New York. And even though Old Hickory had not been regarded as popular in New England, the largest crowds in history greeted him when he reached New Haven and Boston. Harvard gave the President an honorary degree, although John Quincy Adams protested that the university would disgrace itself by honoring "a barbarian who could not write a sentence of grammar and hardly could spell his own name." Although Adams himself had been President, he could not accept the idea that it was the President who was being honored, and not Andrew Jackson.

Early Presidents found it a thrilling experience to hear the applause of their countrymen. They derived great satisfaction from knowing that their every word would be widely printed, and that every thought that they expressed would exert influence. In fact, Theodore Roosevelt once referred to the Presidency as a "bully pulpit" from which to mold public opinion. As Washington, Monroe, and Jackson made their nationwide tours by coach, they were seen and heard by crowds that totaled hundreds of thousands. Theodore Roosevelt and other Presidents who traveled across the nation by special train reached far larger audiences than their predecessors ever did. Today Presidents log thousands of air miles on one official tour, and may be seen by millions of Americans in the course of a single day.

Improved methods of transportation magnified the importance of the President of the United States by bringing him into wider contact with the American people, and exalting his person as the symbol of the nation. Radio made the President the best-known figure on the national scene. Television further personalized the Presidency and made Americans aware of the influence that the Chief Executive exerts on their daily lives.

While in office, the President dominates the news. When he leaves office, he continues to influence political affairs— sometimes as an "elder statesman," sometimes as a powerful force in his own party. And when a President or former President dies, he becomes the central figure in a final, impressive drama.

The funeral of a President or of an ex-President has always been the occasion for an outpouring of public grief, as well as for a review of the glorious past. This is particularly true when the President has met death by assassination. As Lincoln's body was taken from Washington to Springfield, Illinois, the funeral train moved slowly, and halts were made in important cities in order to allow the people of the United

States maximum opportunity to view the remains of their fallen chief. The funeral of John F. Kennedy was another solemn spectacle that moved millions of Americans. The nation mourned in unison because the funeral ceremonies were televised.

Recent Presidents have had a part in planning their own funerals. Together with members of his family and close friends, the President decides upon the kind of service he wishes. Then specialists work out plans for the President's last rites in vast detail. When former President Truman saw the elaborate charts, graphs, and maps drawn up for his five-day state funeral, he reportedly chuckled. "I just hate that I'm not going to be around to see it because it looks like a fine show." The former President had expressed the wish for a simple funeral, but the nature of the office that he had once occupied dictated otherwise. In death, as in life, the President of the United States belongs to the people who choose him as their leader.

## THE CHIEF ATTRACTION OF THE PRESIDENCY

The President of the United States is highly paid, enjoys a princely lifestyle, is unrivaled as the center of attention, and in death receives the homage of his countrymen. But authorities on the Presidency do not consider these attractions of office as the chief reasons why so many Americans want to be President above all else. Most would-be Presidents have considered the advantages so far described as the outward trappings, the mere surface of the prize they seek.

The real lure of the Presidency is the power that the office bestows. Executive authority was impressive when Washing-

**THE HAZARDS OF THE PRESIDENCY.**   Presidents live dangerous lives. Four Presidents have been assassinated, and attempts have been made on the lives of several others. The photograph *(above)* depicts one of the most solemn events in American history, the funeral of John F. Kennedy, thirty-fifth President of the United States, who was assassinated in 1963. Hundreds of thousands of people watched the procession in Washington, while millions saw the ceremony by means of television. *(U.S. Army Photograph)*

ton served as President. Since that time, the Presidency has developed into the most powerful office in the world—the natural goal of anyone ambitious to wield enormous authority. Washington was President of a nation having about 4,000,000 people. Today, the President is the leader of more than 200,000,000 Americans. In Washington's administration, the entire executive branch of government consisted of the President, Vice-President, four department heads, and a few clerks. At present, the executive department has almost 3,000,000 employees, a number equal to three fourths of the total population of the United States in Washington's time. As commander in chief of the armed forces, Washington did not have a standing army, and the few vessels under his command could hardly be called a navy. Today the President as commander in chief directs military forces totaling more than 2,500,000 men and women who staff the world's largest and most formidable navy and air force, and one of the world's largest and most potent armies. In Washington's day, the federal government owned little property and had little money to spend. Today the federal government owns 500,000 buildings, 380,000 motor vehicles, 46,000 airplanes, and 900 ships. It spends more money in *one day* than it spent during Washington's *eight years* as President.

This brief recital underlines the physical basis of the vast power exercised by the President when he directs the operation of the federal government. It is this aspect of the Presidency that Theodore Roosevelt had in mind when he said that "it is fine to feel one's hand guiding great machinery." Contrasting the physical aspects of government in Washington's time and at the present also calls attention to the growth of executive might as the result of the increase in population and the expansion of the economic and military power of the United States. Equally important in bringing about an expansion of presidential authority has been the ascendancy of the federal government over the states, and the emergence of the United States as a world power. The latter development has been particularly important. As commander in chief of the armed forces, the President has conducted the numerous wars in which the United States has engaged. As director of foreign affairs, the President has attempted to prevent war and to make peace when conflicts have terminated. As sole possessor of these enormous powers, the President of the United States has become a towering figure at home and abroad. A former aide of President John F. Kennedy made this point in a recent article. According to Arthur Schlesinger, Jr., in issues of war and peace, the President is the most absolute monarch among the great powers of the world, with the possible exception of the leader of the People's Republic of China.

In a later chapter, the presidential powers cited here will be described at some length, along with other aspects of executive authority. But enough has been said to explain why many ambitious Americans covet the almost unlimited authority vested in the President of the United States. Any citizen who gains this highest of elective offices has the opportunity to mold events, not only in his own nation but throughout the world. To join the ranks of Washington, Jefferson, Lincoln, Wilson, and other venerated Presidents is the goal that any dedicated, ambitious citizen can have in mind when he decides to risk everything in quest of the Presidency. For no other person in the world has greater opportunity to achieve fame, and no other person can do more to benefit mankind. Woodrow Wilson called attention to this unparalleled opportunity when he said that once the President wins "the admiration and confidence of the country, no other single force can withstand him. . . . His office is anything he has the sagacity and force to make it. . . . The President is at liberty, both in law and conscience, to be as big a man as he can."

# III

# WHO MAY BE
# PRESIDENT?

"Be good, little boy. Work hard, and some day you can be President!"

For many years, that promise was part of American folk-lore. The idea that anyone might rise from the ranks of the lowly to the highest position in the nation seemed to be the essence of democracy. But the advice given small boys was never based on hard fact, and as the years passed, the falsity of the pronouncement became more apparent. The truth is that very few Americans qualify for the Presidency. Some are barred because of limitations imposed by the Constitution. Far more are disqualified by the unwritten rules that govern the choice of presidential candidates.

The Constitution imposes only three limitations on would-be Presidents, the first of them having to do with place of birth: "No person except a natural-born citizen" is "eligible to the office of President." Alone among federal offices, the Presidency and Vice-Presidency are restricted to native-born citizens of the United States. (It goes without saying that all the written and unwritten rules that govern the choice of President apply with equal force to the Vice-President. This is in recognition of the fact that the Vice-President is the "heir apparent.") Although senators, members of the House of Representatives, and Supreme Court justices may be naturalized citizens, the President and the Vice-President must be citizens from birth. In other words, in order to qualify for presidential office, a person must have been born within the United States or certain of its possessions, or have been born overseas of American parentage.

In restricting the Presidency to natural-born citizens, the Founding Fathers indicated their belief that a foreign-born Chief Executive might have an unconscious attachment to his native land, whereas a native-born President would be completely American in outlook.

The Constitution imposes a second restriction on presidential aspirants: no person is eligible for the office until he has reached the age of thirty-five. Although a number of the Founding Fathers had not attained that age when they took part in the Constitutional Convention, they agreed that the President should be a mature person. And so while setting twenty-five as the minimum age for a representative and thirty for a senator, the President was required to be at least thirty-five when he came to office.

Actually the age limitation has been of little consequence. Only one presidential candidate of a major party has ever been nominated while in his thirties: William Jennings

Bryan, whom the Democrats nominated as their presidential candidate in 1896 when he was thirty-six. The youngest President to *assume* office was Theodore Roosevelt, who was forty-two when he became Chief Executive upon the assassination of William McKinley in 1901. The youngest President *elected* to that office was John F. Kennedy, who was forty-three when he was inaugurated in 1961. Most Presidents have been in their fifties when elected; several have been in their early sixties. The oldest Chief Executive to assume office was William Henry Harrison, who died at the age of sixty-eight, exactly one month after his inauguration in 1841.

The third constitutional restriction is in the form of a statement that to be eligible for the Presidency a person must have been "fourteen years a resident within the United States." Like the age requirement, this restriction has had little bearing on the selection of presidential candidates. The years of residency have seldom constituted an issue, and when mentioned, have had no apparent influence on the nomination and election of a President. One of the few instances was in 1928, when Herbert Hoover was a leading contender for the Republican nomination. Hoover had spent much of his adult life abroad, first as an engineer and then as administrator of the American relief program in Europe at the end of World War I. But the Republicans dismissed the idea that the Constitution stipulated fourteen years of *continuous* residence in the United States prior to election. They nominated Hoover, and the voting public elected him President. Now that thousands of Americans spend a good part of their lives abroad in some form of government service, the residence requirement set forth in the Constitution has been even more broadly interpreted than in the days of Herbert Hoover.

## SOME UNWRITTEN RULES

Conditions imposed by the Constitution have been of minor significance in determining the occupants of the White House. It is the unwritten qualifications that largely decide the choice of presidential candidates. Even though the Constitution disqualifies no one on the grounds of sex, over half the population of the United States is virtually eliminated as presidential timber because party leaders, the vast majority of whom are men, refuse to consider women as major contenders. This was shown in 1964 when Senator Margaret Chase Smith of Maine entered the Republican presidential primaries, saying that she wanted to show that a woman should be and could be a member of a presidential ticket. The reaction to Senator Smith's candidacy was hostile among some Republican leaders, while most of them displayed indifference. At the national convention of her party, Senator Smith received only 27 of the 1,308 votes cast.

Despite tradition, there is considerable reason to believe that women will become major contenders for the Presidency and Vice-Presidency in the near future. The number of women attending college rose sharply after World War II, and the percentage of women in the labor force also increased dramatically. Both developments were responsible for more intelligent, more aggressive participation in public affairs by women. The League of Women Voters, the National Organization of Women, and other activist groups have participated widely in political reform while membership in consumer-oriented organizations, such as Common Cause and Public Citizen, also has enabled thousands of women to acquire political skills. As women have become more politically adept, men have increasingly accepted members of the opposite sex as their equals in party matters.

Recent reforms have given women a larger role in state and national party organizations, and they constitute an increasingly large bloc of delegates at presidential conventions. Women are nominated for and elected to major executive offices at the local and state levels. In fact, the election of a woman mayor no longer attracts attention, having become commonplace. The voters of New York chose a woman as lieutenant governor in 1974, and in that same year Connecticut elected a woman governor. Two years later, Dixy Lee Ray, former head of the Atomic Energy Commission, was elected as governor of the state of Washington. These successes at the polls have caused political forecasters to predict that one of the major parties would soon choose a woman as its vice-presidential candidate. The next step would be the nomination of a woman as the Republican or Democratic candidate for President.

A second unwritten rule has so far barred nonwhite Americans from being named as the presidential candidate of a major party. This restriction presently eliminates some twenty-five million Americans of African and Asian lineage as contenders, and makes it unlikely that either a Spanish American or an American Indian will be a presidential candidate in the immediate future. But some political scientists note a relaxation in the unwritten rule that major officeholders must be Caucasian. In part, the change has come about because a number of party leaders no longer

**CHOOSING A PRESIDENTIAL CANDIDATE.**   Party conventions name candidates from a small segment of the population because of written and unwritten rules. The choice has become wider in recent years because of the decline of prejudice, but discrimination is still practiced, particularly against women and members of minority groups. In this drawing, the Democrats are shown as they met in New York in 1868 to choose Horatio Seymour as their presidential candidate. *(Courtesy of the Library of Congress)*

accept a restriction that is so flagrantly discriminatory. Of greater influence has been the vast increase in the political activity of minority groups in recent years. For instance, black Americans not only vote in great numbers; they also hold key posts in major parties and occupy public office throughout the United States.

While it may be some years before a major party nominates a nonwhite presidential or vice-presidential candidate, signs point in that direction. Several prominent black leaders have been proposed as the vice-presidential candidate of one of the major parties. In 1968, delegates to the Democratic national convention from the District of Columbia offered a black minister as a presidential nominee. Although he received only a handful of votes at the convention, his nomination was considered a warning that black Americans reject unwritten rules that discriminate against members of their race.

In 1974, black candidates were elected to a number of high executive offices. The voters of Los Angeles, Detroit, Cincinnati, Newark, and Atlanta elected black mayors. Black candidates captured the lieutenant governor's office both in Colorado and California. These victories in major states seemed to indicate that it would not be long before a black American would occupy a governor's mansion, probably in a northern or western state having a large nonwhite population. A development of that sort would increase the likelihood that a major party would nominate a black Vice-President from a pivotal state—that is, a populous state where the major parties are evenly divided, and where a minority might swing an election. Once elected, a black Vice-President might very well succeed to the Presidency. Moreover the election

43

of a black Vice-President would increase the possibility that one of the major parties would nominate a nonwhite presidential candidate—if not an Afro-American, then a Spanish or Asian American. Observers found reason for that belief in several victories scored in the 1974 election. Both Arizona and New Mexico elected Spanish American governors, while Hawaiian voters chose a Japanese American as their chief executive.

## MATTERS OF ANCESTRY AND RELIGION

Since the United States became a nation, almost fifty million immigrants have arrived in this country from all parts of the world. But in all that time, no President has ever been elected whose ancestry was other than western European. Two Presidents—Hoover and Eisenhower—were of Swiss and German descent. Three—Van Buren and the two Roosevelts—were considered Dutch in derivation. All other Presidents have been descendants of immigrants from the British Isles.

Historians have accounted for the disproportionate number of Anglo-Saxon Presidents in various ways. The United States began as a British colony, and it received not only its language but its political institutions from the mother country. In the first century of the republic, the vast majority of its immigrants came from the British Isles and other parts of western Europe. These early immigrants adjusted rather easily to a system with which they were already somewhat familiar, and further strengthened the Nordic character of the United States.

But in the last century, immigration from western Europe has been small when compared with the tide of people coming from eastern and southern Europe, Latin America, and Asia. While the United States is still English in language, Americans of British descent no longer constitute a majority of the population. In fact some experts say that Americans whose ancestors came from any part of western Europe may now be in the minority.

For many years, Americans of western European descent retained control of the socio-economic and political institutions of this country. But after the Civil War, Americans whose ancestors came from other parts of the world constituted an ever larger percentage of the total population. Great numbers of these "new" Americans became successful in politics and other phases of the national life. First at the local level, and then at the state and national levels, they challenged the Nordic American's monopoly of political power. Today mayors with Italian, Polish, Czech, Russian, and Spanish surnames are common.

A notable political event occurred in 1968, when the Republicans nominated a Greek American as their vice-presidential candidate. Spiro Agnew not only was elected, but he was reelected in 1972. He was considered to be the most likely Republican presidential nominee in 1976, until he resigned in disgrace in 1973. Although Agnew was forced from office, some political analysts maintained that his attainment of the Vice-Presidency has made it easier for other Americans of southern or eastern European background to become President or Vice-President. Logically the nomination of presidential candidates whose ancestors came from some Latin American, Asian, or African country could then be expected.

For more than a century after the United States became a nation, the great majority of its people were Protestant in religion. But beginning in the 1870s, the distribution of the American people according to their religion began to change. Of the millions of immigrants who poured into the United States from southern and eastern Europe, a large part were Roman Catholic, Eastern Orthodox, or Jewish in faith. Religious patterns in the United States have continued to change as immigration from eastern and southern Europe has been augmented by an influx of people from Latin America and Asia. While Protestants still constitute a majority of the Americans who profess some religious faith, the Roman Catholic church is the single largest denomination in this country. Jews, Muslims, and Buddhists constitute a small but growing non-Christian minority, and almost every other world religion has adherents in the United States.

In view of the great religious diversity of the American people, one would expect the Presidents who have held office to reflect that fact. On the contrary, of the thirty-eight men who have served as Presidents of the United States, thirty-four have been Protestants; one was a Roman Catholic; and three were members of no church, although their background was Protestant. Most of the Presidents not only have been Protestants; they also have belonged to relatively few of the many Protestant sects. Ten have been Episcopalians, seven Presbyterians, four Unitarians, three Methodists, and three Baptists.

Until 1928, no Catholic or Jew had been named as the presidential candidate of a major political party. As a result, the belief developed that Protestants had a monopoly on the White House. That belief was strengthened by the election of 1928, when the Democrats chose Alfred E. Smith, a Roman

Catholic, as their presidential candidate. His subsequent defeat was widely attributed to his religion. (A number of historians have observed, however, that Smith's defeat had explanations other than religion. The former governor of New York was a liberal Democrat who was unpopular with the conservatives in his party, and Smith opposed Prohibition, while thousands of southern Democrats were ardent Prohibitionists.)

A generation after Smith's defeat, the Democrats nominated another Roman Catholic—John F. Kennedy—to be their presidential candidate, and his victory was cited as proof that the American people had grown more tolerant. Although the outcome of the 1960 election seemed to prove that there was no longer an unwritten rule against nominating members of religious minorities, political analysts pointed out that many Americans still vote in accordance with their religious affiliations. For that reason, party leaders have shown a tendency to pair Catholics and Protestants on their presidential–vice-presidential tickets.

## RESIDENCE AS A PRESIDENTIAL FACTOR

The Presidents of the United States have been male in sex, white by race, western European in ancestry, and with one exception, Protestant in background. Moreover they have come from a small number of states, rather than from many. When classified by place of birth, eight of the thirty-nine Presidents have been natives of Virginia, seven of Ohio, four of New York, three of Massachusetts, and three of North Carolina. Of greater political importance is the list of states

47

in which the Presidents were living when elected. Of the thirty-nine Chief Executives, eight have been residents of New York, six of Ohio, five of Virginia, four of Massachusetts, and three of Tennessee. Of the twenty-two Presidents who have served since the Civil War, eleven came from either New York or Ohio. Only three Presidents have ever been elected from states west of the Mississippi: Hoover from California, Truman from Missouri, and Lyndon Johnson from Texas.

The mode of electing the Chief Executive explains in good part the advantage that some states have in becoming "mother of Presidents." The peculiarities of presidential elections will be considered in the next chapter. Here it is enough to note that residents of certain states are far more likely to be nominated President than the residents of others.

The great majority of Presidents not only have come from a few of the states, but most of them have been drawn from a particular socio-economic class. For one thing, most Presidents of the United States have been far better educated than the average American of their generation. Twenty-nine of the thirty-eight men who have served as President attended college, and twenty-three of them graduated. Of the Presidents who have held office since 1900, only Harry Truman was not a college graduate. Political analysts predict that future Presidents will be drawn from the ranks of college graduates, as they have been in the past. A well-educated politician will continue to have an advantage over his less-educated rivals. For one thing, voters recognize that the skills required of Presidents are now greater than in the past. And since a large segment of the general public is now col-

A DAY OF TRIUMPH.  For almost 150 years, a President elected in November did not take office until the following March. With the adoption of the Twentieth Amendment in 1933, the inauguration was moved to January 20, thus making "lame-duck" Presidents a thing of the past. According to custom, the outgoing President (Buchanan in the illustration) accompanies the incoming President (Lincoln) to the Capitol for the inaugural ceremony. After the Chief Justice of the United States administers the oath of office, the new President assumes his duties. (From Harper's Weekly, 1861, courtesy of the New York Public Library)

lege-trained, voters can be expected to raise the qualifications they seek in presidential candidates.

Presidents have not represented a cross section of the American people as far as education is concerned. They have been even less representative as to occupation. By profession, twenty-six of the thirty-nine Presidents have been lawyers, although not all of them practiced after completing their legal training. The disproportionate number of Presidents who were lawyers is typical of government in general. The great majority of senators and representatives have always been lawyers; members of that profession almost monopolize the judicial system; and they occupy strategic posts in all federal administrative and regulatory agencies.

Few Presidents have come to that high office without considerable experience in some phase of government. In fact, all recent Presidents have spent almost their entire adult lives in government service. Twenty-two Chief Executives served in the armed forces. Twelve of them were generals, although only four—William Henry Harrison, Zachary Taylor, Ulysses Grant, and Dwight Eisenhower—were considered professional soldiers. Fourteen Presidents once served as governors of states, while four were military or territorial governors. At the federal level, eighteen Presidents once served in the House of Representatives, and sixteen in the Senate. Eight were members of a prior Chief Executive's cabinet, in most instances as secretary of state. Thirteen Presidents were Vice-President before assuming the higher office.

Serving as secretary of state was considered the best stepping stone to the Presidency in the early days of the republic. In a later period, occupancy of the governor's mansion of a

populous state was regarded as a likely prelude to occupancy
of the White House. Since World War II, the Senate has
been the major vantage point from which presidential
campaigns have begun. Of the last seven Presidents, four
served as senators prior to their nomination. A fifth President,
Gerald Ford, had been a member of the House of Representatives.

When considered as individuals, the Presidents of the
United States display great diversity. In physical appearance,
they have run the gamut—from James Madison, who was
five feet four inches tall and weighed not much more than
100 pounds, to Abraham Lincoln, who towered over most
of his countrymen at six feet four inches, and William
Howard Taft, who tipped the scales at 332 pounds. Andrew
Johnson was largely self-taught, and earned his living as a
tailor, while Woodrow Wilson received a Ph.D. degree and
earned his living as an author and college president. Thomas
Jefferson spoke so poorly in public that he wrote his State
of the Union messages and had them read to Congress. In
contrast, Franklin D. Roosevelt was a spell-binding orator
who welcomed the opportunity to address Congress in person
and to speak to the American people on a nationwide radio
hookup.

But the diversity of the Presidents is perhaps more apparent than real, considering the fact that they have been
drawn from a rather small segment of the general population. The written and unwritten rules discussed in this
chapter have confined the choice of presidential candidates
to a rather select few. A composite portrait of the likely presidential nominee of a major party would be of a natural-born
white male citizen residing in a populous state east of the

Mississippi. The typical nominee of a major party would be of Anglo-Saxon ancestry, Protestant in religion, a college graduate, a lawyer by profession, and either the governor of a state or a member of Congress.

This description obviously applies to only a very small number of people living in the United States. From this select few, each major party selects its standard bearers—one as its presidential candidate, the other as its vice-presidential nominee. The method of selecting two presidential candidates from more than 200,000,000 Americans is described in the chapter that follows.

# IV

# MAY THE BEST
# MAN WIN

It was 3:00 A.M. Eastern Standard Time, but from the Atlantic to the Pacific, Americans were still sitting in front of their television sets, watching the most spectacular late-late show on record.

No one was more interested in what he saw on the television screen than the chief of the United States Secret Service. His home in Washington was connected by direct wire to two platoons of Secret Service operatives—one stationed at Hyannisport, Massachusetts, the other in Los Angeles. From time to time the chief talked with the inspectors at their posts on opposite sides of the continent. Like millions of their countrymen, the Secret Service agents were following the election returns, waiting to learn who the next President of the United States was to be. Once the winner became apparent, the Secret Service would establish security by throwing an invisible, protective wall around the President-elect.

Even before the polls closed that night of November 8, 1960, political experts had predicted a tight race, but few had forecast a photo-finish. As the early morning hours ticked on, first John F. Kennedy, the Democratic candidate, and then Richard M. Nixon, the Republican nominee, established a narrow lead. But at 5:35, the chief of the Secret Service learned that Kennedy had carried Michigan, which put him over the top. The chief called the inspector in Hyannisport, and within minutes the Secret Service platoon had secured the compound where various members of the Kennedy family had their homes.

The United States had a new President, but he had won by a hairbreadth. Of the approximately 68,000,000 votes cast, Kennedy's margin was only 114,000—a victory of two tenths of one percent.

In 1960, it was Richard Nixon who lost by "a nose." Eight years later, the same presidential candidate won by a nose— 43.42 percent of the popular vote to his Democratic opponent's 42.72 percent. The 1976 presidential election proved to be yet another "cliff hanger," when Jimmy Carter, the Democratic nominee, edged out his Republican opponent, Gerald Ford, by less than three percentage points in a stirring election that brought almost eighty million Americans to the polls.

The three elections were the closest in recent presidential history, but a number of other contests have aroused intense interest. In fact, every four years the American people expect to witness a battle royal, as candidates fight for the highest office that the nation can bestow. Years before the campaign begins, would-be Presidents make the White House their goal. Months before the convention opens, presidential candidates meet with their lieutenants and map the strategy to be used in capturing the party nomination. Meanwhile public-relations counselors, television experts, fund raisers, speech writers, and other specialists are planning the spectacular event that a presidential election generally proves to be.

A year or more before the conventions meet, the national committee of each party chooses the city where delegates will assemble to decide upon their candidate for President. The convention city must have a good transportation system, ample hotel facilities, and an auditorium large enough to accommodate fifteen or twenty thousand delegates and spectators. Party conventions attract great numbers of people who spend money freely. For that reason, businessmen may offer a national committee half a million dollars or more to make their city the convention site.

A national committee, which is made up of one man and one woman from each state, not only chooses the convention city but it also determines the number of delegates that each state may send to the party gathering. At one time, it was a simple matter to set the quota for each state. The figure was double the combined number of its senators and representatives. But fixing the number of delegates from each state became complicated, once the Republicans introduced a system for rewarding party success at the polls. Under the "bonus" plan, each state continued to have its basic representation at the national convention. But states that elected

Republican candidates to major offices were awarded additional delegates at the next national convention. After the Republicans adopted the bonus system, the Democrats followed suit. As a result, recent party conventions have been very large. The Democrats convened in New York City in July 1976 with 3,008 delegates in attendance. When the Republicans met in Kansas City in August of that year, 2,259 delegates were on hand to nominate the presidential candidate of their party.

The delegates who represent their states at the national convention are chosen by either a party election or a party convention. Each system for selecting delegates has many variations. For example, in states using the convention method, the process of selecting delegates may begin at the local level, where party members meet as a caucus to choose delegates to the district convention. At the district level, delegates to the state convention are chosen. In turn, the state convention names the delegates who take part in the national convention. Some states have a more simplified system than the one outlined above; others use a more complicated method.

The state convention may agree on a slate of delegates that are pledged to one presidential candidate; the delegation may be divided between two or more contenders for the presidential nomination; or the state delegation may not be committed to any candidate. Sometimes a state convention selects a slate of delegates who are pledged to support the presidential candidacy of their governor or one of their United States senators. This "favorite son" candidate is ordinarily not a major contender for the nomination. He controls a bloc of votes, however, and may exercise considerable influence by swinging his support behind a leading presidential candidate at the crucial moment.

All the more populous states and a number of the smaller ones now choose delegates to the national conventions by means of primary, or party, elections. Like party conventions, primary elections differ from state to state. There are, however, two principal methods of selecting delegates to the national convention. In some states, delegates are directly elected by party members. These delegates may be pledged to a particular presidential candidate, or they may be uncommitted. In other states, party members choose delegates by indicating their preference for one of the presidential candidates whose name appears on the primary ballot.

Primary elections differ not only as to type but also in their importance. For some time, the first presidential primary in an election year has been that of New Hampshire. Even though New Hampshire sends relatively few delegates to the national conventions, presidential candidates campaign strenuously in that small state. A victory in the first presidential primary influences voters in the other party elections that extend from February to June. Candidates also concentrate their attention on the states that send large numbers of delegates to the national convention of their party. Nine states—California, New York, Pennsylvania, Illinois, Ohio, Michigan, Texas, New Jersey, and Massachusetts—have as many delegates as the other forty-one states combined, which explains their importance in the eyes of politicians.

Primary elections have become increasingly important in

deciding who will be President of the United States. In the 1976 election, almost three fourths of all delegates to the Republican and the Democratic conventions were elected at the presidential primaries held in the various states. Primary elections have lessened the influence of party bosses by widening participation in the selection of presidential nominees. At one time, presidential candidates were named by party leaders who controlled the blocs of delegates sent to national conventions by local and state machines. The hold of political bosses was strengthened by the fact that individuals and organizations that received favors from the machine contributed large sums of money to candidates who had been hand-picked by party leaders.

Before the 1976 presidential campaign, Congress made important changes in the way that primary campaigns are financed. Under the old system, candidates for the nomination of their party depended entirely upon private financing. That is, the money used by the candidate was his own, or else it was contributed by interested individuals and organizations. In most cases, the funds came from a few large contributors who expected some favor in return should "their" candidate become President. The new law reduced the influence of interest groups and wealthy individuals by placing a ceiling on the amount of money that any contributor can give. On the other hand, the law encouraged many small contributors to support a candidate. This was accomplished by offering federal funds to match those raised by the candidate in small amounts from many people living in a number of states. The federal matching funds now make it possible for a little-known candidate to campaign on a more equal footing with a well-known candidate who has the support of a powerful organization of businessmen, labor leaders, or other interest group.

## A YEAR OF SURPRISES

The increasing importance of primary elections has made it necessary for presidential hopefuls to plan their strategy long before the national convention. This political development became evident in 1976—a year of political surprises. At the beginning of the year, it was generally assumed that the Democrats would have the usual "brokered" convention. In other words, when the delegates to the party convention assembled, no candidate would already have a majority of the votes pledged to him. That being the case, the Democratic nominee would be selected by "horse trading" among the delegates pledged to the various candidates for the nomination. But contrary to all predictions, one of the Democratic presidential contenders had the nomination "sewed up" before the convention opened.

The manner in which Jimmy Carter, the peanut farmer from Georgia, made himself the Democratic presidential candidate has been described by *The New York Times* as one of the most brilliant political maneuvers in American history. The success of the former governor underlined the importance of primary elections and made it certain that future presidential candidates would carefully study the strategy used by an underdog to win his party's nomination

Most Democrats did not regard Carter's candidacy very seriously because he was a southerner—and neither major party had nominated a candidate from the Deep South in more than a hundred years. Moreover he had never held national office, which was generally considered essential for a presidential candidate. But even though the Georgian was something of an outsider, he had several advantages over his rivals. He launched his campaign early with the assistance of skilled aides who were willing to devote their lives to making Jimmy Carter the President of the United States. The former governor also was fortunate in having a wife who was an able campaigner, and many relatives who promoted his candidacy.

Carter was wealthy enough to finance his campaign at the beginning, and he could devote his full time to electioneering. This gave him an advantage over the other contenders for the Democratic nomination. Most of them were United States senators or state governors who were tied down by the offices they held. Carter entered all the presidential primaries but one, unlike his rivals who entered only those primaries where they thought that they would make a good showing. The primary elections quickly brought the Georgian to the attention of voters throughout the nation. This exposure was widened by extensive use of television including a simultaneous appearance on the three major networks to an estimated audience of forty-three million Americans of voting age.

Party leaders watched in amazement as the self-assured Georgian took the lead in securing delegates. He picked up delegates in almost every election, and the reverses that he suffered in some primaries were more than offset by notable victories in other states. One by one, the rival contenders for the Democratic nomination dropped out of the race. When it became apparent that Jimmy Carter was the certain nominee of his party, almost everyone tried to jump on the

Georgian's bandwagon as it rolled toward the Democratic convention.

The Republican primary elections of 1976 were no less surprising than the Democratic contests proved to be. At the beginning of the year, political forecasters predicted that the Republicans would settle upon their presidential nominee before the national convention opened. That seemed to be the standard pattern for Republican conventions. It appeared even more certain that the Grand Old Party would follow its usual custom because the Republican who was then the occupant of the White House sought his party's nomination.

But the forecasters were as wrong about the Republican primaries as they were about the contest for the Democratic nomination. President Ford's right to the Republican nomination was challenged by Ronald Reagan, the former governor of California. The defender was in a somewhat weak position because he was the first President who had been appointed to his high office, rather than having been elected to it. (In accordance with the Twenty-fifth Amendment, President Nixon had named Ford, then minority leader in the House of Representatives, to be Vice-President, when that office was vacated in 1973 by the resignation of Spiro Agnew. After Congress confirmed the appointment, Ford became Vice-President, and when Nixon resigned in 1974, Ford succeeded him as President, as provided in Article II of the Constitution.)

As the President and his challenger campaigned across the nation, the contest resembled a horse race in which two leaders run neck and neck over the course. All eyes focused on the finish line: the Republican national convention. Before President Ford gained his photo-finish victory, millions of Americans who watched the spectacle had learned a great deal about party conventions.

## CIRCUS, HORSE RACE, OR RIOT?

The expensive, strenuous, and long-drawn-out process of choosing presidential nominees reaches its climax at the national convention. This gathering of party representatives is a peculiar feature of American government. Because a party convention is a colorful, noisy, and unpredictable affair, writers sometimes describe it as a combination circus, horse race, and riot.

The convention is dominated by party leaders, among them the chairman of the national committee. Presiding over the tumultuous assembly is the convention chairman, who must be highly skilled in parliamentary procedure. Frequently he is the Speaker of the House of Representatives or a former Speaker. The keynote speakers are the orators of the day, and they arouse a great deal of enthusiasm by denouncing the opposing party and praising their own leaders and policies.

The convention committees are of considerable importance. As its name indicates, the Rules Committee determines the procedure under which the convention operates. The Resolutions Committee meets before the convention and draws up the party platform, which outlines general policy and lists objectives. Once the Resolutions Committee has agreed upon the various "planks" of the platform, it is submitted to the convention for debate and final adoption. A third committee of the convention passes on the credentials of delegates when they are disputed. For instance, in 1952, Texas, Louisiana, and Georgia each sent two slates of delegates to the Republican convention—one supporting Dwight D. Eisenhower and the other supporting Robert A. Taft. A bitter fight developed between the Taft and the Eisenhower forces. Eventually the Eisenhower delegates from the three southern states were seated, which ended Taft's hopes of securing the nomination.

The convention rank and file is made up of delegates from the fifty states, the District of Columbia, Puerto Rico, and several territories of the United States. In recent years, efforts have been made to increase the representation of women, young people, and minorities. Nevertheless, studies of the 1972 and 1976 Republican and Democratic conventions indicated that most delegates belonged to the upper middle class, and that women, minority groups, and young people were still underrepresented.

The major contenders for the presidential nomination are known months before the convention opens. Their candidacies do not become official, however, until the clerk calls the roll of the states, inviting the delegates to offer their nominees to the convention. At one time, nominating speeches were long and flowery, and each was accompanied by a noisy demonstration. Democratic conventions were particularly notable for their endless speechmaking and for their bitter quarrels. In an effort to correct past abuses, the Democrats recently adopted rules that limit nominating and seconding speeches. The new regulations are also designed to keep controversies from reaching the convention floor.

When all candidates have been nominated, the voting begins. More often than not, the outcome of the voting is a foregone conclusion because one candidate has captured a majority of the delegates at the state conventions and in the primary elections that precede the national convention. But if the leading contenders must fight for the nomination after the convention opens, great excitement develops among the delegates. They are courted by lieutenants of the candidates, and are offered various inducements to win their support. Much of the "horse trading" takes place on the convention floor. The conferences held by party leaders in the famous smoke-filled rooms of hotels and clubhouses are even more influential in determining the outcome of the balloting. However, the deals once made by party bosses have become more difficult to carry off, now that convention proceedings are televised.

Conventions sometimes become deadlocked because neither of the leading contenders is able to secure a majority of the vote. When that happens, the delegates choose a "dark horse" as candidate—someone who had not previously been considered a presidential contender. James K. Polk (1844) was the first "dark horse" to gain the Presidency, and James A. Garfield (1880) and Warren Harding (1920) were later Presidents who came to office by that route.

Having named its presidential candidate, the convention turns to the selection of his running mate. Actually, delegates have little responsibility for the vice-presidential nomination because presidential nominees now choose their own running mates, and the convention merely approves. This was made clear at the 1964 Democratic Convention when President Lyndon Johnson, after holding the nation in suspense for weeks, dramatically announced that Senator Hubert Humphrey was his choice for Vice-President.

The presidential nominee considers several matters when he makes his choice of a running mate. The person's physical and mental health, political background, reputation, and appeal to voters are matters of concern. In making his decision, the presidential nominee tries to balance the ticket. This means that if the presidential candidate lives in one section of the United States, he is likely to choose a running mate from another part of the country. For example, Kennedy of Massachusetts chose Johnson of Texas as the Democratic vice-presidential candidate in 1960. That same year, the Republican presidential nominee, Nixon of California, chose Lodge of Massachusetts as his running mate. Healing party differences may be another goal in naming the vice-presidential candidate. Thus the runner-up for the presidential nomination may become the vice-presidential choice, or a conservative presidential nominee may select a liberal member of the party to balance the ticket.

The care that recent Presidents have exercised in choosing their running mates reflects a new attitude toward the Vice-Presidency. As the 1976 election approached, political commentators pointed out that each of the last three Presidents, four of the last six, and six of the fifteen Presidents in the twentieth century had earlier served as Vice-President. Political commentators reminded voters that every Vice-President is only a heartbeat away from the Presidency. And as the Twenty-fifth Amendment (1967) provides, the Vice-President may become head of the government of the United States under circumstances other than the death of the President. The Vice-President succeeds to the Presidency when the President resigns or is removed from office—the circumstance that developed when Richard Nixon resigned his office in 1974 and was succeeded by Gerald Ford.

The Vice-President also may assume presidential authority

under another unusual set of circumstances. When the President's physical or mental health makes it impossible for him to conduct the affairs of his office, the Vice-President may take over. But to guard against any effort to remove the President for purely political reasons, the Twenty-fifth Amendment describes the procedure to be used in determining the incapacity of the Chief Executive. (Another provision having to do with presidential succession is a law providing that the Speaker of the House of Representatives is next in line to the Vice-President, and following him comes the president pro tempore of the Senate. After that come members of the cabinet, beginning with the secretary of state.)

## THE GREAT CAMPAIGN

The acceptance speech that a presidential candidate makes when he receives his party's nomination marks the beginning of the great campaign. This important address outlines the candidate's major objectives and indicates the sort of campaign he can be expected to wage. Those who are interested in finding out the direction in which the party is headed generally place more reliance on the candidate's speeches than on the platform adopted at the convention.

No other country equals the United States in the time devoted to choosing its Chief Executive. Counting primary campaigns, the process of selecting the President requires almost a year. The final lap—the period between Labor Day and the first Tuesday in November—is the most crucial. The candidates exert their maximum effort, and the voting public displays its greatest interest.

66

The first presidential campaigns were quiet and genteel when compared with later contests. Until 1840, presidential candidates regarded campaigning as somewhat undignified. But supporters of William Henry Harrison, the Whig candidate of 1840, changed the character of presidential campaigning. The Whigs adopted a catchy campaign slogan— "Tippecanoe and Tyler Too!"—and made a log cabin their symbol. They organized torchlight processions that attracted thousands of people, who were then encouraged to sing the Whig campaign songs and to drink the hard cider that was freely distributed. Harrison was swept into office, which caused his defeated opponent, Martin Van Buren, to complain that he had been "lied down, drunk down, and sung down."

Presidential campaign managers have shown great skill in attracting crowds to hear their candidate. Supporters of Stephen Douglas were the first to hire a campaign train (1860). The candidate's arrival in town was announced by firing a cannon that had been mounted on a flatcar. But once candidates were able to use airplanes, campaign trains became a thing of the past. Radio and television brought even greater changes in campaigning. William Jennings Bryan, the famed orator who was three times the Democratic presidential nominee, once made twenty-four speeches in that many hours. During the 1896 campaign, he spoke to record audiences that totaled more than five million people. In contrast, a presidential candidate on a nationwide television hookup may now speak on a single occasion to an audience of fifty million people.

As he campaigns, a candidate deals with the issues that he and his advisers consider of particular concern to voters.

"TIPPECANOE AND TYLER TOO". The Whig Party worked a great change in politics when it conducted the first well-organized, loud, and rough presidential campaign in 1840. Its candidate was William Henry Harrison, the hero of the battle of Tippecanoe, and the campaign featured hard cider, music, and a log cabin. *(From a drawing by John Wolcott Adams, reproduced from the collection of the Library of Congress)*

The successful campaigner tailors his remarks to his audience. President Truman showed particular skill in adapting his speeches to differing audiences as he campaigned across the United States in 1948. He concentrated on labor-management relations in industrial Michigan; stressed farm issues in his tour of the Midwest; discussed civil rights in New York, with its powerful bloc of black voters; and focused on hydroelectric power in the Northwest, a region of mighty rivers.

Presidential candidates sometimes avoid discussing issues because they are bound to offend many voters once they take a stand. Instead the candidate's chief objective may be to create a favorable image in the eyes of voters. He tries to develop the picture of an honest, friendly, and intelligent person who will serve the interests of the American people. This attempt to create a favorable impression, rather than to deal with the problems of the day, concerns authorities on government. They believe that many voters are persuaded to cast their ballots for the candidate who looks best on the television screen, rather than the one who best deals with issues. Political scientists are also critical of voters who are overly impressed with the way candidates rate in the public-opinion polls that have become a feature of presidential campaigns. Critics of these ratings believe that many voters "jump on the bandwagon," rather than make up their own minds about a candidate.

Television hookups, chartered jets, and the services of public-relations experts are now considered necessary features of presidential campaigns. The use of such facilities made the 1952 presidential campaign the most expensive then on record. But the $11.8 million spent that year was a

CAMPAIGN LITERATURE. Political parties make frequent use of the flag and other patriotic symbols when they advertise and take the credit for economic and political success at home and abroad. In this campaign poster, President McKinley's bid for reelection is based upon the claim that he led the nation from poverty to prosperity during his first term of office. *(Courtesy of the Library of Congress)*

**ELECTION NIGHT.**    Since presidential elections usually are hard fought, they create great interest throughout the nation. Until the advent of radio and television, the center of any major city was crowded on Election Night, when returns were projected onto a screen set high above the street. Downtown New York is the scene of this study, drawn in 1888, the year tha⁻ Benjamin Harrison was elected President. (*From* Harper's Weekly, *reproduced from the collection of the Library of Congress*)

71

small amount when compared with the $24.8 million spent in 1964, and the $95.2 million spent in 1972. Most political scientists were not critical of the *amounts* spent in behalf of presidential candidates because the total sum is small when compared with the amount of money spent annually in the United States on candy, chewing gum, and soft drinks. But political scientists were very critical of the *sources* of the campaign money. Most of the funds spent by both major parties came from a few wealthy individuals and a few giant organizations. These large contributors gave money to presidential candidates because they expected some favor in return. For example, a wealthy man or woman might contribute several hundred thousand dollars with the promise of being named an ambassador. A labor union might donate several million dollars to a candidate with the expectation of having a friend in the White House. A business organization might make an equally large contribution in the expectation of receiving favored treatment once the candidate was elected.

The growing influence of selfish interests in determining the outcome of presidential elections finally caused Congress to act. After the 1972 election, the laws governing national campaign expenditures were changed. In effect, Congress reduced the role of wealthy contributors and increased the role of government. The object was to make presidential elections more democratic by having great numbers of Americans finance campaigns, rather than having a few people underwrite the cost. This was brought about by inviting everyone who pays a federal income tax to make a small contribution to the presidential campaign fund. A minimum of $20 million is paid from this fund to each of the major parties for use by their presidential candidate. The amounts that minor parties receive are determined by their showing at the polls. To qualify for public funds, candidates must agree to spend no more than the amount of money received from the federal government, to accept no private contributions, and to report all campaign expenses to the Federal Election Commission. Congress placed a ceiling on the amount of money that national committees may spend in behalf of their presidential candidates, and outlined the conditions under which labor unions, business organizations, and other interest groups may promote a presidential nominee's candidacy.

## THE FINAL BATTLE

The manner in which presidential elections are conducted is greatly influenced by a peculiar feature of American government: the Electoral College. As noted in Chapter I, the framers of the Constitution provided for the indirect election of the President, rather than having him directly elected by popular vote. The Constitution authorizes each state to select the same number of presidential electors as it has United States senators and representatives. These electors meet in their respective states and cast their vote for President. The electoral votes are then forwarded to Washington to be counted in the presence of Congress.

The Founding Fathers intended the Electoral College to consist of well-informed men who would have one objective: to select the best-qualified candidate as President of the

United States. But political parties developed during Washington's first term of office. Thereafter electors were always chosen on the basis of their party membership.

The Electoral College now operates in this fashion. The District of Columbia is assigned three electors, and the fifty states have from three to forty-five electors each, depending upon their population. Electors are chosen at state primary elections, party conventions, or meetings of the party committee. Americans who go to the polls to cast their ballots for a presidential candidate are actually voting for those electors who are pledged to him.

An unwritten rule—"winner takes all"—largely determines the outcome of a presidential election. Under this system, the candidate who receives the greatest number of popular votes in a state wins all its electoral votes. For example, in the presidential election of 1960, Kennedy carried Hawaii by only 115 votes, yet he received all 3 of its electoral votes. Nationwide in the popular vote Kennedy won by "a nose," yet he received 303 electoral votes to his opponent's 209. (There is one exception to the winner-takes-all rule. Maine awards 2 of its 4 electoral votes to whichever presidential candidate carries the state as a whole. The other two electoral votes go to whoever wins each of the state's two congressional districts.)

Presidential candidates concentrate their money and their time in the states that have the most electoral votes. California, for instance, has 45 electoral votes, which makes it equal to twelve of the small states with the District of Columbia thrown in for good measure. Of the populous states, the most important are the pivotal ones, such as New York, Pennsylvania, Ohio, and Illinois. These are populous states in which the two major parties are somewhat evenly balanced. By swinging one of these pivotal states, a candidate captures a sizable number of electoral votes to add to those gained in states that are considered safe for his party. For example, a Democratic presidential candidate counts on winning a majority of the popular vote in Massachusetts because his party almost always carries that state. His popular majority will give him all the electoral votes of Massachusetts. He does less campaigning there and spends less money in that sure state than he does in Illinois, which has more electoral votes, and which has a record of voting sometimes for a Democratic candidate and sometimes for a Republican.

In order to be elected President, a candidate must secure a majority of the 538 electoral votes. Although presidential elections frequently are very close, the operation of the winner-takes-all rule generally gives one of the two major candidates a rather lopsided victory. On the rare occasions where there are three or more major candidates, one of them is likely to be elected by a plurality. That is, one candidate gains his victory by receiving more of the popular vote than any of his rivals, but less than a majority. In 1912, for example, Woodrow Wilson received approximately 42 percent of the popular vote, while his two major opponents, Theodore Roosevelt and William H. Taft, totaled more than 50 percent of the popular vote between them. Yet Wilson became President, having won 435 of the 531 electoral votes. In addition to the Presidents elected by a plurality of the popular vote, three Presidents—John Quincy Adams, Rutherford B. Hayes, and Benjamin Harrison—received fewer popular votes than their leading opponent.

75

The President is not officially chosen until the electors meet in their respective state capitals in mid-December. While electors are expected to vote for the candidate to whom they are pledged, there is no federal law binding them. Unless state law requires electors to honor their pledge, they may vote as they choose. In 1960, 1968, and 1972, a delegate rejected the party nominee to whom he was pledged, and voted for another person.

Should no presidential candidate receive a majority of the electoral vote, the House of Representatives elects the Chief Executive from among the three highest contenders. The Senate determines the outcome of a vice-presidential contest. In such cases, senators vote as individuals, but members of the House vote by state, with each state casting a single ballot. Congress was first involved in the election of a President in 1800, owing to the original stipulation of the Constitution that the candidate receiving the greatest number of electoral votes would be President, while the second highest would become Vice-President. A tie between Thomas Jefferson and Aaron Burr resulted in Jefferson's election by the House of Representatives—and the prompt amendment of the Constitution to provide for the separate election of President and Vice-President. In 1824, the presidential election was again thrown into the House, this time because none of the four major candidates received a majority of the electoral vote. John Quincy Adams emerged victorious, even though he received fewer electoral votes than Andrew Jackson.

One of the gravest crises in American history occurred after the election of 1876. The Democratic candidate, Samuel J. Tilden, received a majority of the popular vote and the

76

A DANGEROUS ELECTION.  In 1876, contested election returns delayed the selection of the President while tension mounted in the nation. Only a few days before Inauguration Day the next Chief Executive was named by a committee set up by Congress. In this drawing, United States senators are shown entering the House of Representatives with the electoral returns from the various states. *(From* Leslie's Illustrated Weekly, *1877, reproduced from the collection of the New York Public Library)*

undisputed right to 184 electoral votes, just one short of the majority needed to make him President. The Republicans challenged Tilden's right to the 20 electoral votes of South Carolina, Florida, and Louisiana by claiming fraud. Congress was called upon to settle the dispute, but it was in no position to act because the Senate was controlled by the Republicans, while the Democrats controlled the House of Representatives. The deadlocked Congress established a commission to decide which candidate would receive the disputed electoral votes. The fifteen members of the commission reached a decision on strictly party lines, with the eight Republicans deciding in favor of their candidate, Rutherford B. Hayes, by giving him all 20 disputed electoral votes. Only two days before the President was to be inaugurated, was his name announced to the American people, who had been in suspense for weeks. Tilden's supporters were outraged by the decision, and some hotheads wanted to raise an army and force the inauguration of their candidate. But Tilden discouraged such projects, and left to historians the privilege of referring to the "stolen" election of 1876.

The method used to elect the President has been criticized since the early days of the republic. For one thing, the Electoral College system enables candidates with a minority of the popular vote to capture the Presidency. And delay, deadlock, and political deals are a possibility when the House of Representatives must elect the President—as the crises of 1800, 1824, and 1876 proved. Public-opinion polls indicate that a large majority of the American people favor the popular election of the President, and in 1969 the House of Representatives voted for a constitutional amendment to make that possible. The proposed amendment was rejected by the Senate, however, and advocates of the direct election of the President were discouraged by the setback. But shortly after he assumed office in 1977, President Carter gave his powerful support to a constitutional amendment that would do away with the Electoral College and permit the American people to choose their Chief Executive by direct election. President Carter asked Congress to approve the proposed amendment by the necessary two-thirds majority of both houses, and to submit it to the states. Political analysts predicted that widespread popular support for the direct election of the President would cause a minimum of three fourths of the states to ratify the amendment, as required by the Constitution.

Major changes in the method of electing the President already have been brought about by constitutional amendment. A good example is the Twelfth Amendment, which provides for the separate election of President and Vice-President. The Twentieth Amendment outlines the procedure to be used when a President-elect dies before Inauguration Day, has not been selected by that time, or has failed to qualify. The amendment also bestows on Congress broad authority to act, when due to other unusual circumstances the nation approaches Inauguration Day without a President. But political scientists often point out that it is impossible to foresee and to plan for every crisis that may develop in the Presidency. The people of the United States, acting through their Congress, will have to deal with difficult situations as they arise. Judging by the way in which past crises have been handled, the future is secure.

# V

# THE FAITHFUL
# EXECUTION
# OF THE LAW

President Jackson had an important decision to make. At stake were the lives and property of thousands of Indians. Also involved was the honor of the United States government. Moreover relations between the executive and the judicial branches of government demanded consideration. And as a further complication, Jackson had to take American public opinion into account.

The fateful decision that Andrew Jackson had to make concerned the Cherokee Indians of Georgia. The independence of the Cherokee nation had been guaranteed by the United States in a treaty signed in 1791. Led by the great Sequoyà, the Cherokees had developed a written language, established schools, built roads, and set up a democratic form of government. They welcomed Christian missionaries, and otherwise adopted European ways. No one could call the Cherokees uncivilized.

But the vast tract of rich, cultivated land held by the Cherokee nation was coveted by the white settlers who surrounded it, particularly after gold was discovered in the area. The state government of Georgia demanded the removal of the Cherokee Indians beyond the Mississippi, so that white settlers could have their land.

President John Quincy Adams (1824–1828) had stationed federal troops in Georgia to protect the Indians under the terms of their treaty with the United States. But Adams was a President from a northern, seaboard state. His successor, Andrew Jackson (1828–1836), was the first President from a frontier state, where Indians generally were regarded as natural enemies. Jackson withdrew the soldiers from the Indian lands, thus putting the Cherokees at the mercy of the white settlers.

In an effort to prevent the expulsion of the Indians, a white missionary instituted court action, and the case went before the Supreme Court, whose Chief Justice was the famed John Marshall. The Court ruled that the laws of Georgia had no force within Cherokee territory, thus upholding the treaty between the Indians and the United States.

All eyes now turned to Andrew Jackson. As President, the Constitution obligated him to "take Care that the Laws be faithfully executed." Defenders of Indian rights believed that those words meant upholding the treaty between the United States and the Cherokee nation. This belief was reinforced when the Supreme Court handed down its decision. In effect, that ruling reminded the President of his duty to enforce the law.

But Andrew Jackson did not regard the treaty as binding. He not only declined to enforce the Supreme Court decision, but is reported to have said of the Chief Justice, "John Marshall has made his decision. Now let him enforce it."

A number of historians have dealt harshly with President Jackson because he failed to uphold the treaty between the United States and the Cherokee nation. Others have pointed out that Jackson could not have been expected to protect Indians because he had conducted military campaigns against them. Various writers have defended Jackson by saying that the President regarded the removal of the Cherokees from Georgia as the only way to save them from extermination.

But while historians may differ as to the reasons for Jackson's Indian policy, they agree that his decision determined the fate of thousands of native Americans. For when President Jackson failed to execute the terms of the treaty with the Cherokees, he made the loss of their land inevitable. The Cherokees were forced to take "the trail of tears"— from Georgia to Oklahoma—a cruel migration that cost thousands of lives and caused bitterness that has lasted to this day.

President Eisenhower (1952–1960) was confronted with a difficult decision. The rights of millions of Americans were at stake. The delicate relationship between the federal government and the governments of the various states was a matter that the President had to consider. And because the people of the United States were sharply divided on the issue confronting the President, whatever he decided to do would anger a vast number of his countrymen.

The fateful decision that President Eisenhower had to make concerned all black Americans in general, and the black schoolchildren of Little Rock, Arkansas, in particular.

Three years before, the Supreme Court had handed down one of the most important decisions in its history: *Brown* v. *Board of Education of Topeka* (1954). In that historic ruling, the Court unanimously declared that racial segregation in public schools was unconstitutional. The decision aroused a storm of protest in states that by law maintained two public school systems, one for blacks and one for whites. Public officials in states that maintained segregated school systems not only denounced the Supreme Court's interference in their affairs, but they resisted, particularly when federal courts throughout the South followed up the *Brown* decision with orders that required local school systems to desegregate.

President Eisenhower had not been happy with the Supreme Court's decision that outlawed segregation in public schools because he regarded it as too drastic. And as the governors of some of the southern states began to organize resistance to federal court orders, the President realized that a confrontation between the government of the United States and the governments of several states was likely. The prospect filled him with uneasiness.

But the issue was joined when the federal court for the eastern district of Arkansas ordered the school board of Little Rock, the state capital, to desegregate its public schools.

The governor of the state ordered units of the Arkansas national guard to prevent black children from attending Little Rock High School.

Once again, civil rights leaders called upon a President to

"take Care that the Laws be faithfully executed." But demands upon the President to enforce the Supreme Court ruling were countered by demands, both in the North and in the South, to refrain from meddling in state affairs.

After consultation with his advisers, the President acted. As commander in chief of the armed forces of the United States, he federalized the Arkansas national guard, thus removing it from the governor's control. Then he ordered military units to Little Rock to protect those black children who planned to attend previously all-white schools. For the first time since Reconstruction, federal troops were sent to the South to enforce national law.

Having acted, the President went before the American people on a radio-television hookup to explain why he had taken such extreme measures: "Whenever normal agencies prove inadequate to the task, and it becomes necessary for the Executive Branch of the Federal Government to use its powers and authority to uphold the Federal Courts, the President's responsibility is inescapable. In accordance with that responsibility, I have today issued an Executive Order directing the use of troops under Federal authority to aid in the execution of Federal law. . . ."

The President was as strongly condemned as he was praised for his policy. But no one doubted that the show of federal force in Arkansas was almost as far-reaching in effect as the Supreme Court ruling that prompted it. The Eisenhower decision was another milestone in the long road toward racial equality in the United States.

These dramatic examples of executive action emphasize the role of the President as the chief law-enforcement officer of the United States. The President, however, seldom needs to take such drastic measures. Most laws that Congress enacts and most decisions handed down by the federal courts are not challenged. In fact, most laws are more or less self-executing. That is, once Congress has enacted legislation and provided machinery for its enforcement, the law is carried out in routine fashion. The President is seldom called upon to take action.

But the President does influence the day-by-day enforcement of the laws of the United States by paying particular attention to certain pieces of legislation, while showing little or no interest in others. To explain this statement, one would have to point out that through the years Congress has placed thousands of laws on the statute books. Some of these laws have been enacted at a President's insistence. He regards them as important, and after their enactment sees that they are vigorously enforced. Or the President may show concern for legislation enacted during previous administrations, and decide to enforce with vigor certain laws that some of his predecessors more or less ignored.

By concentrating attention on certain types of legislation, a President places a distinct stamp on his administration. For example, both President Coolidge and President Hoover believed that "the business of the United States is Business." For that reason the two Republican Presidents gave particular attention to laws that protected and promoted business. On the other hand, another Republican President, Theodore Roosevelt, was regarded in some quarters as an enemy of business because he vigorously enforced laws designed to curb unfair practices.

In enforcing the laws of the United States, the President

uses a number of devices, of which physical force is the most seldom employed. The President rarely has to resort to the use of federal marshals or units of the armed forces, largely because the great majority of the American people are law-abiding. They are willing to accept, however grudgingly, the laws made by the members of Congress whom they elect. The President's enormous prestige also makes many reluctant citizens accept an unpopular law, particularly when he explains the necessity for the legislation on a nationwide television hookup, and then appeals for cooperation. Some Americans who would like to challenge a particular law are restrained by the knowledge that even though the President and his subordinates ordinarily use the "velvet-glove" system of law enforcement, they will employ the "iron hand" if need be.

## THE PRESIDENT AS BUSINESS MANAGER

The framers of the Constitution gave Congress the responsibility for making the laws of the United States, and authorized the federal courts to interpret those laws when they were disputed. The President was assigned the task of carrying out the policies laid down by the lawmaking branch of the government. The Founding Fathers recognized that the manner in which Chief Executives carried out the intent of Congress would determine the character of American government. In that respect, the President was made the keystone of the political system described in the Constitution.

The President's role as the chief law-enforcement officer of the new republic was a primary concern of the Founding

Fathers. They did not foresee an equally important presidential responsibility: his management of the largest business in the world. This powerful role developed because of social and economic changes that took place in the United States after the Constitution was adopted. The American people crossed the Appalachians, then the Mississippi; reached the Rockies, then the Pacific; and finally acquired territory overseas. Americans developed the most productive agricultural system in the world, and then made their country the leading industrial power. This economic might enabled Americans to change their weak, almost defenseless nation into the greatest military power ever known to man. Accompanying those vast economic and political developments were social changes that transformed the daily lives of the American people. Among the most notable of these developments was the urbanization of the United States.

The developments noted above have brought about change in the federal government, particularly in the executive branch. During the administration of George Washington, the legislative, executive, and judicial branches had few employees because the federal government was a limited operation. But each of the social and economic changes mentioned above has created governmental problems. Americans have come to expect their government to deal with such matters as land settlement, road and canal building, protection from foreign competition, labor-management disputes, and economic depression. Congress has met the demand for government assistance by developing a program and creating an agency to carry it out. Almost all these new divisions of government have been placed under the direction of the

President. As a result, the executive branch of government now overshadows Congress and the federal courts in the number of its employees and in its field of operation. Congress and the offices directly responsible to it have approximately 39,000 employees, while the federal court system employs about 9,000 men and women. In contrast, the executive branch has almost 2,800,000 employees, a number roughly equal to the population of Los Angeles.

The President of the United States now has the responsibility of managing the biggest business in the world—the federal government. Whereas the president of a giant corporation, such as American Telephone and Telegraph or General Motors, supervises several hundred thousand employees, the President of the United States oversees the work of millions of men and women. And while the president of a major corporation directs the expenditure of hundreds of *millions* of dollars, the President of the United States draws up a budget calling for the expenditure of hundreds of *billions* of dollars. In other words, quite apart from his duty to see that federal law is enforced throughout the United States, the President has the responsibility of overseeing the day-by-day operation of the vast, complicated machinery of the executive branch of the government.

## THE MANAGEMENT TEAM

The elaborate structure of the executive branch of government is shown in the chart on page 92. That highly complex organization is based upon grants of authority made in Article II, Section 2, of the Constitution.

The Founding Fathers created several other executive offices, the most important of them being the Vice-Presidency. Of course, that was not the view of John Adams, the first man to hold the position. After a short time in office, the Vice-President wrote to his wife, Abigail, that "my country has in its wisdom contrived for me the most insignificant office that ever the invention of man contrived or his imagination conceived." John Adams resented the fact that he actually had no real executive power. And while he presided over the Senate, and might break a tie vote, he was largely a figurehead. In the opinion of John Adams, the Constitution made the Vice-President a nobody.

The Vice-Presidents who succeeded John Adams often expressed their unhappiness in occupying such a powerless position. But while the Vice-President has often been called the "forgotten man of American government," his role is highly important. In the first place, he is the "heir apparent," who may at any moment become the Chief Executive upon the death, resignation, or removal of the President. Nine Vice-Presidents have become President by that route. Moreover, the Vice-President of the United States occupies a strategic position from which to seek the Presidency by election. By utilizing his opportunity to cultivate party leaders, familiarize himself with the executive branch of government, and become known to people at home and abroad, the Vice-President may assure himself of the presidential nomination of his party. (Since 1960, six of the ten presidential candidates of the major parties have been former Vice-Presidents.)

The Constitution gives the Vice-President no executive duties, and most Presidents have not seen fit to share author-

PRESIDENTIAL POWERHOUSE. The Oval Office of the White House is the nerve center of the government of the United States. The most sophisticated communications system in the world connects the Chief Executive's private office with all parts of the globe, and decisions made in the White House are quickly transmitted to the President's subordinates wherever they are stationed. This cutaway view of the White House shows

the rooms on the lower floors that are open to the public, including the state dining room on the left and the East Room (where formal events are held) on the right. The upper floors are the private quarters of the presidential family and members of the household staff. *(Copyright by the White House Historical Association, photograph by National Geographic Society)*

# THE EXECUTIVE BRANCH OF GOVERNMENT

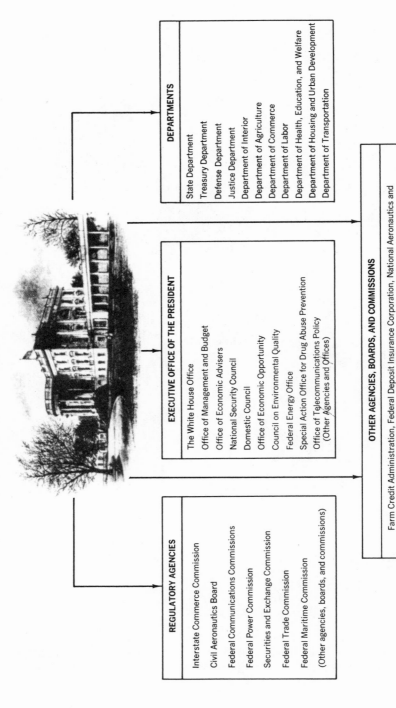

## REGULATORY AGENCIES

Interstate Commerce Commission

Civil Aeronautics Board

Federal Communications Commissions

Federal Power Commission

Securities and Exchange Commission

Federal Trade Commission

Federal Maritime Commission

(Other agencies, boards, and commissions)

## EXECUTIVE OFFICE OF THE PRESIDENT

The White House Office

Office of Management and Budget

Office of Economic Advisers

National Security Council

Domestic Council

Office of Economic Opportunity

Council on Environmental Quality

Federal Energy Office

Special Action Office for Drug Abuse Prevention

Office of Telecommunications Policy

(Other Agencies and Offices)

## DEPARTMENTS

State Department

Treasury Department

Defense Department

Justice Department

Department of Interior

Department of Agriculture

Department of Commerce

Department of Labor

Department of Health, Education, and Welfare

Department of Housing and Urban Development

Department of Transportation

## OTHER AGENCIES, BOARDS, AND COMMISSIONS

Farm Credit Administration, Federal Deposit Insurance Corporation, National Aeronautics and Space Administration, National Labor Relations Board, Veterans Administration.
(Consult U.S. Government Organization Manual for completed list of Federal executive agencies.)

ity with their Vice-Presidents. But several Chief Executives have elevated their Vice-Presidents to a position of influence by making full use of their services. For example, during William McKinley's first term, he gave his Vice-President so many duties that Garret Hobart was often referred to as the Assistant President. Richard Nixon assigned Vice-President Agnew a key role in policy making. The Vice-President was sent on fact-finding trips for the President. When Agnew made public statements, he was regarded as a spokesman for the President. In fact, the President was accused of having his Vice-President offer any criticism that he knew would antagonize a large number of people. In that way, Vice-President Agnew was both a mouthpiece and a shield for President Nixon.

The framers of the Constitution created in the Vice-Presidency an executive office that normally plays a minor part in the operation of the government. But the Founding Fathers devised another kind of executive office that has had an important function from the beginning. This is the executive *department*, of which there were originally four and are eleven at present. Their chief purpose is to assist the President in directing the day-by-day affairs of the federal government. For example, Washington's secretary of state, Thomas Jefferson, conducted foreign affairs according to the President's wishes. The secretary of the treasury, Alexander Hamilton, was responsible for managing the finances of the new republic. The secretary of war, Henry Knox, was in charge of national defense, while the attorney general, Edmund Randolph, was the President's chief lieutenant in law enforcement, as well as his legal adviser.

The heads of the executive departments of government are

(From E. B. Fincher, The Government of the United States, 1976, reproduced by permission of Prentice-Hall, Inc., Englewood Cliffs, N.J.)

appointed by the President, with the consent of the Senate, and may be removed by the President when they no longer enjoy his confidence. The names of the executive departments indicate the nature of the programs that they administer. Each department has a number of divisions, all of them headed by an official who is responsible to the secretary.

When the heads of the executive departments meet with the President as a group, they form his cabinet. Although the cabinet is not mentioned in the Constitution, it developed in Washington's first term of office and has been an important feature of American government ever since. Some Presidents have relied heavily on their cabinets. President Polk, for example, laid most important policies before his cabinet and encouraged full discussion. Sometimes he called for a vote on an issue and made the cabinet decision his own. Several Presidents more or less bypassed their cabinets, while others have sought advice but rejected it. Thus on one famous occasion, Abraham Lincoln asked his cabinet's opinion on a decision that he was about to make. Every member of his cabinet advised against the proposed action. After listening politely, Lincoln announced, "One aye, seven nays. The ayes have it." In this way, he emphasized the fact that ultimate executive decisions are the President's alone. Or, as bluntly stated on the placard that President Truman kept on his desk, "The Buck Stops Here."

Even though Presidents may not seek the advice of their cabinets, or may fail to follow advice when given, they frequently rely on some member of the cabinet for counsel. Alexander Hamilton exerted such influence over President Washington that he was resented by many Americans. President Franklin Pierce's attorney general, Caleb Cushing, an-

94

THE ASSISTANT PRESIDENT.   No First Lady was more influential than
Eleanor Roosevelt. Her crippled husband, Franklin Delano Roosevelt, sent
her on missions throughout the world, and reporters, photographers ·and
cartoonists delighted in recording the extraordinary variety of her activities.
Here the President's wife is shown with young Americans at a military
canteen during World War II. *(Office of War Information, 1944, reproduced
from the collection of the Library of Congress)*

95

nounced that he would make his post "the great, controlling, supervising office of the Administration"—a promise that he carried out, thus making so many enemies for Pierce that the President was not renominated by his party. More recently, President Eisenhower followed, seemingly without question, the advice on foreign affairs that was given by his secretary of state, John Foster Dulles.

Besides the departments mentioned above, Congress has established other types of executive agencies to assist the President in managing the affairs of the nation. A number of these agencies were set up for the purpose of regulating a particular industry that affects the well-being of a great number of people. For example, the Interstate Commerce Commission regulates railroads, buses, and pipelines. The Federal Communications Commission lays down rules that hold radio and television networks to certain standards of broadcasting, while the Federal Trade Commission protects consumers by enforcing regulations against unfair or dishonest business practices. Other regulatory agencies are shown on the chart, reproduced on page 92, and their names indicate the matters with which they are concerned.

Regulatory agencies have several members who serve for stated, overlapping terms. Members are named by the President, but they may be removed only for the reasons given in the law that established the agency. In other words, members of regulatory agencies may not be dismissed simply because they have differences with the President. Like an executive department, a regulatory agency has a large number of employees who carry out the policies determined by the governing board or commission.

## THE WHITE HOUSE OFFICE

The Great Depression of 1929–1939, World War II, and post-war developments brought about a sharp increase in presidential responsibilities. As a result, Congress established additional agencies to assist the President in the conduct of his office. A number of these agencies are now grouped in the Executive Office of the President. As the chart shows, this third executive division has several parts. The White House Office is staffed with the President's personal advisers—men and women whom he chooses to help him decide on policies and carry them out. For instance, several of these presidential assistants are in constant touch with key senators and representatives and with the heads of the executive and regulatory agencies. Other assistants prepare presidential messages to Congress and write the speeches that the Chief Executive makes in other places. Several aides handle the President's highly important meetings with representatives of newspapers and television networks. Still others determine which of the many persons who want to talk with the President are actually admitted to his office in the White House.

As its title suggests, the National Security Council is responsible for advising the President on matters pertaining to the national defense and to the military position of the United States throughout the world. The council is made up of high military and civilian officials who assist the President in making long-range plans and who advise him when a crisis develops.

The titles of the other subdivisions of the Executive

Office of the President indicate the responsibilities entrusted to them by the President whom they serve. There is not one phase of national life that does not come under review by the officials of some division of the Executive Office of the President. For that reason, the chart shows more than a complicated organization. It is a reminder of the vast extent of executive power—power that reaches into every home and every business concern in the United States, thus affecting the daily life of every American.

# VI

# THE PRESIDENT,
# THE CONGRESS,
# AND THE COURTS

New Year's Eve, 1932, was not a time for celebration in the United States. In fact, most Americans were fearful of the future. Fourteen million men and women who wanted jobs were out of work, and in some communities more than half the labor force was unemployed. As a consequence, thousands of families were cold and hungry. Farmers were no better off than their city cousins. Crops were bringing prices below the cost of production. Many farmers who could not pay interest on their mortgages had their land taken from them. Banks failed across the nation, causing countless Americans to lose their lifetime savings.

On March 4, 1933, discouraged people who listened to their radios heard a confident, ringing voice telling them that "the only thing to fear is fear itself." The eloquent speaker was Franklin Delano Roosevelt, the President of the United

States who was inaugurated that day. (Later Presidents have been inaugurated on January 20, in accordance with rules laid down by the Twentieth Amendment.)

People who heard the President's speech were inclined to believe him, not only because his bold words sounded convincing, but because they had faith in a man whom a crippling disease had reduced to life in a wheel chair, but who despite that handicap had first become governor of New York and then President of the United States. It was this courageous man who promised to lead his people out of the Great Depression.

The response to the President's nationwide address was overwhelming. Until Franklin Roosevelt assumed office, the White House mailroom ordinarily received a few hundred letters a day, and even an important event rarely brought the figure to 1,000. The new President received more than 450,000 letters in response to his first inaugural address. That deluge of mail marked the beginning of the famous "One Hundred Days," when events moved so fast that Americans had difficulty in keeping abreast of them.

The new President's distant cousin, Theodore Roosevelt, was the first Chief Executive to lay before Congress a well developed legislative program of his own, which he called the "Square Deal." Woodrow Wilson had followed the first Roosevelt's bold example with an even more ambitious program that he labeled the "New Freedom," and pushed Congress hard to enact the laws that he proposed. Franklin D. Roosevelt coined the term "New Deal" for his program, and he applied the lessons learned from his predecessors in carrying out the vast undertaking.

As soon as he was inaugurated, Roosevelt called Congress

into special session and laid before it legislation designed to pull the United States out of the most severe economic depression in its history. All banks in the United States were closed until their soundness was proved, and when they opened, they were subject to regulation and had government guarantees that inspired the confidence of their depositors. The Agricultural Adjustment Act was a far-reaching program designed to raise the price of farm produce. Home owners were protected by government insurance on their mortgages. Several hundred thousand young men were given jobs in the Civilian Conservation Corps. A vast public-works program was established, so that jobless Americans would find employment on dams, roads, schools, hospitals, and other major construction projects. Unemployed writers, artists, teachers, and other "white-collar" workers were employed in government-financed projects of many kinds. And to provide immediate relief to disadvantaged Americans, federal funds were given to state and municipal governments for aiding the poor, the ill, and the handicapped.

The President sent message after message to Congress, urging the prompt adoption of the emergency measures devised by members of his Cabinet and by his "brain trust" —a group of college professors and other thinkers that Roosevelt relied upon for advice. From time to time, the President addressed the American people on a nationwide radio hook-up. In these "fireside chats," Roosevelt took his listeners into his confidence, inspired them, and created a favorable climate for the enactment of the legislation that he wanted. The President not only was an eloquent speaker when he addressed the nation via radio, but he was equally persuasive in dealing with the press. While many Presidents have disliked and distrusted newspaper reporters, Roosevelt enjoyed meeting them. Because his relationship with reporters was so cordial, President Roosevelt usually had newspaper writers on his side, even though newspaper owners generally were hostile to the New Deal.

By vigorously asserting his right to take part in the law-making process, Franklin D. Roosevelt further increased the authority of the Presidency. Historians tend to agree that he placed his stamp on the legislative process as no other President has done.

## PRESIDENTIAL LAWMAKING: PRO AND CON

Franklin D. Roosevelt was one of the most loved and most hated of all Presidents. There were several reasons for the intense dislike that he created. Some of the ill feeling was based on the belief that because he was a champion of the poor, he threatened the privileges of the rich. The President also aroused the opposition of people who regarded him as a threat to the American system of government. These critics reminded their fellow citizens that the Founding Fathers had divided the powers of government into three separate divisions—the legislative, the executive, and the judicial— that offset one another. Critics then pointed out that President Roosevelt had developed his own legislative program and had induced Congress to accept it. Thus the President had become the chief legislator as well as the chief executive, and thereby made himself something of a dictator.

But critics who contended that President Roosevelt had violated a basic principle of American government sometimes overlooked the fact that the Constitution provides Presidents with important legislative powers. President Roosevelt aroused opposition because he used these constitutional powers more vigorously than earlier Presidents had done.

The Constitution requires the President from time to time to give Congress "information of the state of the Union, and recommend to their consideration such measures as he shall judge necessary. . . ." From the administration of Washington onward, Presidents have sent a message to Congress or appeared before a joint session of the Senate and the House of Representatives at the beginning of each year. This State of the Union message is the President's review of national and international affairs, but it is also his plea for action. In other words, he suggests measures that Congress should enact to promote the welfare of the American people.

After giving a rather general idea of national needs in the State of the Union message, the President prepares other statements on specific subjects, the most important of which deals with the national budget. Under the direction of the Chief Executive, each government agency prepares its estimate of funds needed for the ensuing year. These requests for money are studied by officials of the Office of Management and Budget, and if considered proper, are placed in the massive document that the President submits to Congress. The preparation of the national budget allows the President to determine the objectives of the United States to a considerable degree. Thus, by recommending increased appropriations for environmental protection, the President can stress the need for conserving natural resources, or by calling for greater expenditures for mass transportation, the

President may call attention to the plight of the nation's railroads. The budget submitted by the President has great influence over lawmaking because it provides proposals on which Congress acts.

Members of the Senate and the House of Representatives have come to rely upon presidential guidelines when they enact laws. Presidential leadership is most evident when the same political party controls both the executive and the legislative branches of government. As the acknowledged head of his party, the President expects the cooperation of his fellow party members who serve in Congress. Ideally all party members are united in their objective. Ideally lawmaking is simplified because the President can rely on the congressional members of his party to follow his lead. When such harmony exists, the President may have a requested bill drawn up in some executive office and have it submitted to Congress by members of his party. Its enactment is almost certain because of the close relationship between the President and the members of his party who control the Senate and the House.

But the truth is that members of Congress are highly independent in their views on policy and in their actions. Even when they are members of the President's party, they feel free to oppose him. Presidents attempt to win over reluctant senators and representatives by using their powers of persuasion. That failing, they may apply pressure by using some of the tactics described later in this chapter.

The President's legislative hand is strengthened by the system that the Constitution prescribes for electing members of Congress. Representatives are elected by the voters of particular districts within each state, unless the state has only one representative because of its small population. A representative's first loyalty is to the people who put him in office, and for this reason his views on legislation tend to be provincial. That is, a representative ordinarily is more concerned with the way a proposed law will affect his own district, rather than his state or the nation as a whole. Senators are elected by the voters of an entire state, and for that reason they tend to take a broader view of legislation than representatives do.

The President of the United States is elected not by the voters of a single district or state but by the voters of the entire nation. He is the only elected official who can claim to speak in the name of every American. When he goes before Congress and asks for a certain piece of legislation, he can claim to represent the needs of all citizens.

The President's role as spokesman for all the people has become more important with each development in communication. First, newspapers with mass circulation, then radio, and finally television have enabled the President to communicate with millions of people. The feedback from his supporters enables the President to tell Congress what the American people want in the way of legislation.

The Constitution provides the President with the authority to call Congress into special session, a power that various Presidents have used to persuade a reluctant Congress to enact certain legislation. By calling the national legislature into special session, the President focuses attention on specific laws that he wants. He also focuses the attention of the American people on the senators and representatives whom they have elected, by using his news conferences to publicize the delaying tactics of legislators who oppose his program.

## THE APPOINTIVE POWER: A LEGISLATIVE FORCE

The Constitution gives the President the power to appoint a number of federal officeholders, thus providing him with further influence over lawmaking. This comes about because the President ordinarily consults with one or more members of the House and Senate before he names federal judges, attorneys, ambassadors, and other appointive officeholders. Representatives and senators want the President to appoint their supporters to high office because it strengthens their position in their district or state. But the President usually consults only members of his own party, and frequently he wants something in return for giving the congressman's supporter a job. This price may be the senator's or representative's promise to support legislation the President wants.

The appointment to office in return for political support is known as patronage. It is an accepted practice at all levels of government, and has always had its defenders and its critics. The term is often associated with President Andrew Jackson, who was accused of taking as his motto "To the victors belong the spoils." In that instance, the President was criticized for using his appointive powers to reward loyal Democrats. But Jackson also employed patronage to gain support in the Senate and the House of Representatives.

President Lincoln made great use of his appointive powers in his effort to preserve the Union. A famous example will illustrate the point. Lincoln was convinced that the abolition of slavery would give the Civil War the character of a crusade. In that way, he would rally support at home and persuade European statesmen that justice was on the side of the Union. The abolition of slavery required a constitutional amendment, and Lincoln knew that securing such a radical change would be difficult. He counted the states that could be depended upon to ratify the Thirteenth Amendment when it was submitted, and found that the number was one less than required. The President determined to have another state—Nevada—admitted to the Union. But there was considerable opposition to the admission of Nevada, because its distant location and scant population did not seem to entitle it to statehood.

Lincoln was told that Nevada could be brought into the Union only if three key representatives could be persuaded to vote for admission. The President called in one of his aides and told him, "We must carry this vote or be compelled to raise another million men and fight, no one knows how long. It is a question of three votes or new armies. . . . Whatever promises you make, I will perform."

Lincoln's aide called on the three representatives who opposed the admission of Nevada and found that each of them could be won over with the promise of certain appointive jobs for their supporters. The jobs were promised in the name of the President. The three representatives voted for the admission of Nevada. Once admitted to the Union, the state ratified the Thirteenth Amendment, which brought an end to slavery in the United States. The President had employed a dubious method in order to reach a lofty goal.

The use of patronage has been far more often criticized than defended. Civic leaders, Presidents, and members of

Congress have all pointed out the dissatisfaction, inefficiency, and dishonesty that such a practice creates. As a result of widespread criticism of the system, most federal jobs have been placed under civil service. That is, instead of depending upon appointment by the President, most federal employees now secure their positions by passing civil service examinations. Ability, rather than political connections, has become the basis for hiring most federal officeholders. The President appoints relatively few officials, and most of them are either federal judges or law-enforcement officers, or else they are important policy makers within the executive department.

In developing his legislative powers, each aggressive President has applied lessons learned from his predecessors. John F. Kennedy, for example, studied the methods employed by Franklin D. Roosevelt in dealing with Congress, and adapted them to his own purposes. He used his press conferences, television appearances, and speaking engagements to gain popular support for the laws that he wanted Congress to enact. The President's appeals often led many members of his radio and television audience to send letters to their senators and representatives, asking them to vote for the Kennedy-sponsored measures.

Like Franklin D. Roosevelt, President Kennedy sent persuasive messages to Congress, and he went even further than Roosevelt in developing contact with influential lawmakers. Since Kennedy had served in both the House of Representatives and the Senate, he understood the legislative process and made use of this knowledge to further his own measures. He assigned several highly skilled members of the White House staff to maintain contact with the chairmen of con-

**THE PRESIDENT BESIEGED.** According to the Constitution, the Senate must approve a number of the President's appointments to major offices. However, until most positions in the executive department were placed under civil service, the President was required to fill thousands of offices "on his own." As a consequence, job seekers besieged the President and interfered with the conduct of his office. The cartoon above portrays the plight of the incoming President, Benjamin Harrison, in 1889. *(Copyright by White House Historical Association, photograph by National Geographic Society)*

gressional committees. The President also cultivated influential representatives and Senators by telephoning them from time to time, and by inviting them to White House social functions. One of the most effective ways of gaining the support of the senators and representatives in his own party was to assist them in their campaigns for reelection. For instance, the President would make a speech in the candidate's state or district, perhaps at a fund-raising dinner. Meanwhile President Kennedy worked closely with the representatives of organized groups that were interested in legislation that he was urging Congress to adopt. Thus to further his school-construction legislation, he encouraged officials of labor unions to put pressure on their individual senators and representatives.

## THE POWER TO SAY NO

The examples of presidential influence over legislation that have been given so far may be described as positive. In other words, they show the President as the proposer or initiator of legislation. These positive legislative powers are reinforced by negative ones—meaning the President's right to veto laws of which he disapproves. The President's veto power is a good example of the system of checks and balances provided for by the Constitution. When the President vetoes a measure, he returns it to Congress without his signature, generally accompanied by a statement of his objections. Presidents have made increasing use of the veto. Washington vetoed only two acts of Congress in his eight years of office; and Jefferson vetoed none. Franklin D. Roosevelt, on the other hand, vetoed more than six hundred bills. Few presidential vetoes are overriden, since a two-thirds vote in each house of Congress is required.

When the President's party is in a minority in Congress, vetoes are more likely to be overriden. Thus a Republican Congress overrode Democratic President Truman's veto of the key Labor-Management Relations (Taft-Hartley) Act of 1947, while some years later a Democratic Congress overrode a number of Republican President Ford's many vetoes. Because of the difficulty of overriding a veto, the President's threat to veto a measure will sometimes prevent its enactment. Or Congress may modify the proposed law in order to secure the President's signature.

Sometimes the President disapproves of a measure but does not return the bill within the required ten days—Sundays excepted—while Congress is in session. In that case the measure becomes law without his signature. On the other hand, if Congress should adjourn during the ten-day period, a disapproved measure will die for want of the presidential signature. This is known as a pocket veto, and it is final because Congress is not in session and therefore cannot override it.

## THE PRESIDENT AS CHIEF MAGISTRATE

As noted earlier, the Constitution divides the powers of government into three branches: the legislative, the executive, and the judicial. But the Founding Fathers also provided for a system of checks and balances. As we have seen, the President has an important role in the legislative process. And now his judicial powers will be noted.

The President influences the judicial branch of govern-

# GOVERNMENT UNDER THE CONSTITUTION

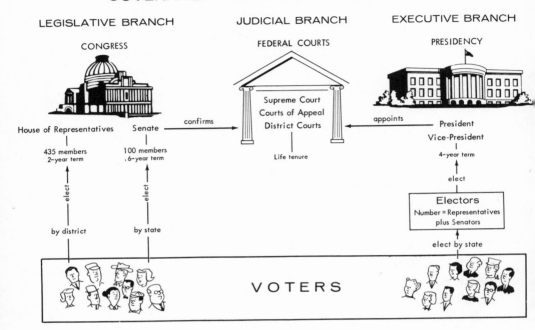

THE PRESIDENT, THE CONGRESS, AND THE COURTS. The system of checks and balances established by the Constitution is shown in this chart. In theory, the three branches of government are coequal. In practice, the President has become the dominant element in the system. *(From E. B. Fincher, The Government of the United States, 1976, reproduced by permission of Prentice Hall, Inc., Englewood Cliffs, N.J.)*

ment because he appoints, with the advice and consent of the Senate, all federal judges and attorneys. (The latter officials represent the government in court proceedings, and oversee the enforcement of federal law.) As a rule, judges are suggested to the Chief Executive by senators or representatives of the President's party, after approval by the bar association of the state in which they reside. But the President reserves the right to examine the record of the proposed judge and to name a jurist who shares his views on government. For example, when President Nixon named Warren E. Burger to be Chief Justice of the United States, it was generally understood that the Chief Executive had purposely chosen a jurist who was more conservative than Burger's immediate predecessor, Chief Justice Earl Warren.

The President has other powers that may be considered judicial in character, since they allow him under certain conditions to set aside federal court decisions. The President may shorten the sentence imposed by a federal judge or require the payment of a fine, rather than imprisonment. The President also has the authority to commute a sentence from death to imprisonment, and he may reprieve a convicted person by postponing punishment until a further investigation can be made. He may pardon a person convicted of a federal crime, thus wiping the slate clean by removing all liabilities resulting from the conviction. The President may grant a blanket pardon or amnesty to an entire group, as illustrated by President Andrew Johnson's amnesty of former Confederate soldiers held guilty of rebellion.

The President uses his powers of pardon, reprieve, amnesty, and commutation only rarely and with great care because they are politically dangerous. That is, when the

President so acts, he is sure to antagonize many people. That fact was made clear when President Ford gave an unconditional pardon to his predecessor, Richard M. Nixon. President Ford acknowledged that the former Chief Executive had "become liable to possible indictment and trial for offenses against the United States." Then President Ford explained that in order to spare his predecessor and the nation further punishment for the Watergate scandal, he was granting "a full, free, and absolute pardon unto Richard Nixon for all offenses against the United States which he, Richard Nixon, has committed or may have committed or taken part in" during his tenure of office.

The pardon raised a storm of protest across the nation. President Ford was denounced by many newspaper editors and television commentators for pardoning Richard Nixon before his guilt or his innocence could be established. A great many members of Congress also criticized the pardon because it came just as the trials of the former President's principal aides were getting underway. These congressional critics charged that President Ford had encouraged the belief that there was a double standard of justice in the United States. The pardon aroused so much opposition that the new President finally offered to appear before the House Judiciary Committee to explain the reason for his action. Since the proceedings were televised, the people of the nation could hear their President offer an explanation for the pardon. The episode offered proof that while the President of the United States may be the most powerful ruler in the world, he can be brought to account by the people who place him in office.

# VII

# FIRST IN WAR,
# FIRST IN PEACE

Even before James K. Polk was elected President (1844), he was convinced that California should be added to the United States. Polk had heard of the riches of California from American sea captains who had put in at San Francisco, and from reports made by John C. Frémont, a young U.S. Army officer who had led an expedition from Missouri to the Pacific coast.

Like many Americans of his day, Polk believed in Manifest Destiny—the conviction that one day the United States would stretch from the Atlantic to the Pacific. The way seemed clear to the President-elect because the area between the western boundary of the United States and the Pacific Ocean was owned by Mexico, a weak, disorganized nation. The danger was that if the United States did not acquire California, it would fall into the hands of the British, the French, or the Russians.

Shortly after he assumed office, President Polk began to encourage the American settlers in California to declare their independence from Mexico—as the Americans living in Texas had done not long before. Polk hoped that an independent California would join the United States, again following the lead of the Republic of Texas. To encourage the Californians to act, President Polk sent Frémont on another expedition to the Pacific coast. He thought that the presence of American forces in the area might promote the movement for independence. Meanwhile President Polk considered other means of extending the territory of the United States.

Mexico had not recognized the independence of Texas. When the Republic of Texas joined the Union in 1845, Mexico protested to the United States and then broke off diplomatic relations. In response, President Polk sent an army under General Zachary Taylor to the Nueces River, which was the southwestern boundary of Texas. But while using his military power to protect Texas from possible invasion by Mexican forces, President Polk tried diplomacy as a means of reaching his objectives. He instructed the American representative to Mexico to "'make a deal." The Mexican government owed a considerable sum of money to American citizens. President Polk offered to cancel those claims against the Mexican government if it would make the Rio Grande, rather than the Nueces River, the boundary between the United States and Mexico. (The Rio Grande is approximately 150 miles south of the Nueces.) The American diplomat was also instructed to offer Mexico $5 million if it would sell New Mexico to the United States, and to offer a larger sum for California.

The Mexican government refused to deal with President

Polk's representative. As soon as Polk received word that his
diplomatic efforts had failed, he exercised his power as commander in chief of the armed forces of the United States.
He ordered General Taylor to cross the Nueces River, the
recognized boundary of Texas, and to march to the Rio
Grande, the boundary that Polk desired. Mexican forces contested the occupation of what they regarded as their soil.

Having received news of the battle, President Polk called
a meeting of his cabinet, and with its help prepared a war
message for submission to Congress. When Congress assembled, it heard the President charge that "Mexico has
passed the boundary to the United States, has invaded our
territory and shed American blood upon the American soil."

At the President's request, Congress declared war on
Mexico.

The Mexican War (1846–1848) was bitterly opposed by
many Americans because they regarded it as an illegal, im-
moral use of force. Some of the sharpest criticism on that
score came from a young member of Congress from Illinois,
Abraham Lincoln. The future President denounced Polk
for sending American troops onto soil that "was not ours;
and Congress did not annex or attempt to annex it." Lincoln
stressed the danger of allowing a President to decide for himself when a neighboring nation should be invaded, and
pointed out that the Constitution grants the power to declare
war to Congress alone.

But widespread criticism did not prevent President Polk
from prosecuting the war with great vigor. As commander
in chief, he chose the generals who conducted the campaigns,
determined strategy, and even concerned himself with matters of detail, such as purchasing mules for the army. As a

result of his efforts, Polk added more territory to the United States than any President but Thomas Jefferson. He left office after only one term, satisfied that he had helped fulfill the prophecy that one day the United States would stretch from the Atlantic to the Pacific and from the Great Lakes to the Rio Grande.

Historians have made much of the vast expansion of American territory that James K. Polk brought about. Political scientists have been interested in Polk because he greatly expanded presidential powers. When he assumed office, Polk announced his objectives, and indicated that he would serve only one term. At the end of his four years as President, Polk could point to the achievement of each of his declared objectives. His success was based not only on the incredible amount of time and energy that he gave to his duties, but also to the bold use he made of his authority. As director of foreign affairs, he showed great skill in dealing with Great Britain in the dispute over Oregon. He managed to add that territory to the United States without war. In fact, the settlement of the Oregon boundary dispute brought about closer ties with Great Britain, at that time the powerful northern neighbor of the United States.

As commander in chief of the armed forces, Polk proved that even though the Constitution gives Congress the exclusive right to declare war, a President may by his actions make such a declaration inevitable. President Polk underlined that fact when he ordered the army to take a position that forced the Mexican government to begin hostilities. Congress had no alternative but to declare war. Polk's generous interpretation of his military powers provided later Presidents with the incentive to use their authority with equal force. As a matter of fact, each wartime President has stretched Polk's concept of his military powers even further.

## LINCOLN'S VIEW OF PRESIDENTIAL POWER

The criticism that Representative Abraham Lincoln directed toward President Polk because of the Mexican War was mild when compared with the criticism leveled at President Abraham Lincoln during the Civil War. Polk escaped the charge of dictatorship, but Lincoln's critics frequently used that term when they denounced what they regarded as the President's unconstitutional acts.

The Union seemed to be falling apart as Lincoln proceeded from Springfield to Washington for his inauguration. Rumors that an attempt would be made on the President-elect's life caused Lincoln to begin the final leg of his train journey at midnight, disguised as an invalid in a sleeping car. When he arrived in the nation's capital, he found everything in confusion. Fear gripped the populace because the Confederate States of America had been proclaimed, and its government was preparing for war. As Lincoln went by carriage from his hotel to the Capitol to take the oath of office, the procession was heavily guarded, and reporters described the inauguration as more like a funeral than a celebration.

In his inaugural address, and in statements made during the following month, Lincoln showed a spirit of conciliation toward the South. But on April 12, 1861, the Confederate States of America fired on Fort Sumter, a federal installation in Charleston harbor. The Civil War had begun. One of the most important chapters in the history of the Presidency also began at that moment. Lincoln did not summon Congress into special session immediately, as many people expected. Instead he asked Congress to assemble on July 4, almost three months after war began.

In the period between the beginning of war and the special session of Congress, Lincoln made one dramatic move after another. Congress had not declared war, but the President ordered the navy to blockade southern ports. He increased the size of the regular army, called out the state militias, spent $2 million from the federal treasury without the authorization of Congress, and pledged the credit of the United States in order to secure a loan.

To discourage pro-Confederate activity within the Union, the President made further use of his authority as commander in chief of the armed forces. He designated several parts of the North as "theatres of war," and made them subject to martial law. He authorized the arrest of suspected traitors, closed the mails to "treasonable correspondence," and suspended the writ of habeas corpus along the line of communications between Washington and New York. Since habeas corpus guarantees the right of an arrested person to be brought promptly before a judge, the suspension of the writ was regarded by Lincoln's critics as an unwarranted violation of civil rights. And to a number of senators and representatives, the President's suspension of the writ was clearly illegal, since the Constitution gives that right to Congress. But Lincoln believed that the Union should be preserved at all costs. Since "these rebels are violating the Constitution in order to destroy the Union," he reasoned, "I will violate the Constitution, if necessary, to save the Union."

By the time Congress met in special session, President Lincoln had placed the nation on a war footing. To bring that about, he had combined his role as commander in chief with his role as "faithful executor of the law." The result was what Lincoln termed his war powers—the authority that enabled him to mobilize the total effort of the nation in order to preserve the Union.

When Congress finally convened, the capital was endangered by a Confederate army just across the Potomac. The hostile forces that were visible from Washington served as a reminder that the Union was threatened from every quarter. A frightened but determined Congress put its stamp of approval on almost every move that Lincoln made. It was sometime later that the President's policies met with congressional opposition, and much later that the Supreme Court passed judgment on certain presidential acts. By that time, Lincoln had successfully staked out a new and loftier claim to presidential power. As he explained to some visitors from his home state, "As commander-in-chief in time of war, I suppose I have a right to take any measure which may best subdue the enemy."

## THE PRESIDENT AND GLOBAL WAR

The military powers that Woodrow Wilson exercised during World War I were far more extensive than those that Lincoln employed to save the Union. For one thing, Wilson directed American participation in a global war, whereas Lincoln's theater of operation was largely confined to the United States. Like Abraham Lincoln, President Wilson named generals and outlined strategy, supervised the creation of a conscripted army and a vastly increased navy, and curbed civil liberties as the sponsor of legislation designed to prevent subversion. But Wilson used his war powers to control the nation's railroads, along with other industries that were vital to the war effort. Before the war was over, the national economy was largely supervised by the commander in chief.

At the outset of the Civil War, Lincoln showed how a President may deal with a threat from within by acting independently of Congress. When war broke out in Europe in 1914, Wilson demonstrated the way a President may meet danger from abroad by working closely with Congress. Wilson attempted to keep the United States out of the war, with congressional approval. He tried to end the conflict by acting as mediator between the warring forces—again with congressional approval. When German submarines continued to sink American vessels, President Wilson protested and finally broke diplomatic relations with Germany, once again with the backing of Congress. But at length, the President called Congress into special session, reviewed his unsuccessful efforts to keep the nation out of war, and denounced the German government as an enemy of democracy. Then he asked Congress to declare war, which it did on April 6, 1917. The almost dictatorial power that Wilson exercised thereafter was derived not only from his position as commander in chief, but also from the authority that Congress delegated to him in its own right.

There are many parallels between World War I and World War II as they affected the Presidency. Like Woodrow Wilson, President Franklin D. Roosevelt kept his nation from becoming involved in the global war that erupted in 1939. But Roosevelt had already become convinced that the United States would be drawn into war because its economic and political interests were threatened by the Axis powers: Germany, Italy, and Japan. Accordingly the President sought to prepare the American people for a shift from peace to war, and to persuade Congress to strengthen the armed forces of the United States in preparation for the inevitable conflict.

Congress declared war on the Axis nations after Japan attacked Pearl Harbor on December 7, 1941. The President immediately began to mobilize the nation for total war, using all his vast power as commander in chief, and all the power over the economy that Congress granted him.

World War II was a far more deadly conflict than World War I. Every nation in the world was directly or indirectly involved, and civilians were engaged, no less than military forces. Armies and navies were larger and equipped with more formidable weapons; air power was a new and terrifying instrument of war; and industrial might was a more important factor than it had been in earlier wars. And toward the end of the conflict, the most destructive of all weapons was introduced by the United States: the atomic bomb. Because World War II was a longer, larger, more deadly conflict than World War I, President Roosevelt was a more powerful commander in chief than Woodrow Wilson had been during the previous war. The control that Roosevelt exercised over the military establishment was almost matched by his control over the industrial system that supplied war materials. By means of censorship and skillfully contrived propaganda, the President exercised vast influence over public opinion. By passing over certain military officers and designating others for positions of command, President Roosevelt determined American strategy, and when he conferred with the leaders of allied nations, he helped to fashion global military objectives. His position as leader of the Free World was based in good part upon the fact that he directed the flow of American supplies to Hitler's foes.

Since World War II, the Presidents of the United States have directed military operations in many parts of the globe. Of these ventures, the longest and most costly in lives and money were the Korean War of the Truman administration, and the Indochinese War of the Lyndon Johnson and Richard Nixon administrations. Yet despite the fact that President Truman directed full-scale military operations designed to halt what he regarded as Communist aggression, war was never declared. In 1950, North Korean forces invaded the Republic of South Korea, which was allied to the United States. President Truman promptly ordered American forces in the Far East to throw back the attackers. The President then called for and received support from the United Nations in the American effort to halt aggression. President Truman called the Korean conflict a "police action," but his critics described it as a full-scale war. They denounced "Truman's War" as a dangerous example of presidential trespassing on the powers of Congress.

The age of undeclared wars continued in succeeding administrations. Both President Eisenhower and President Kennedy intervened in the affairs of the Indochinese people by giving technical and military assistance to the government of South Vietnam. When Lyndon Johnson became President, he used his authority as commander in chief to involve the armed forces of the United States in the Indochinese conflict. Soon the President was directing what proved to be the longest and most unpopular war in the history of the United States, but a war that Congress never declared. The President operated in a manner that his opponents regarded as high-handed, since he concealed the true state of affairs in Indo-china not only from the American people but from Congress itself.

The military policy pursued by President Johnson reached its conclusion during the Nixon administration. As commander in chief, Richard Nixon not only continued to wage undeclared war in Vietnam, but he ordered the invasion of neutral Cambodia to further his military objectives. It was this move by Richard Nixon that spurred his opponents in Congress to curb a President's right to wage undeclared war. The methods used to limit the President's military power will be a principal subject of the next chapter, which deals with checks on the Chief Executive.

## THE DIRECTOR OF FOREIGN AFFAIRS

There are several reasons for focusing attention on the military powers of the President. For one thing, the United States has been involved in some form of war during a large part of its history. In waging either a declared or undeclared war, Presidents are able to increase the power of their office because in time of emergency the nation is willing to accept strong and sometimes dictatorial leadership. Even in time of peace, the President's military power gives him extensive authority over all phases of American life. For example, his role as commander in chief of the armed forces indirectly makes him commander in chief of the far-flung industries that supply the army, navy, and air force. This military-industrial complex, as President Eisenhower called it, dominates the economy of the United States, and exerts a profound influence over research, technology, the mass media, and education. As the key figure in the military-industrial complex, the President of the United States influences the life of every American.

But even though the President's military role is a dramatic one, his role as director of the nation's foreign affairs is no less important. The President is the official spokesman of the United States, a role made clear when he joins other heads of state at "summit" conferences. During World War II, President Roosevelt, Prime Minister Churchill, and Generalissimo Stalin held a number of such meetings to plan strategy. Since that time, summit conferences have been held on many occasions.

The President has the authority to recognize formally the existence of a new nation or a government that has come to power as the result of some kind of revolution in an established nation. For example, after the United States had for many years refused to recognize the existence of a Communist government in Russia, President Franklin Roosevelt in 1933 extended recognition to the Soviet Union. The President's recognition of a new nation or a new government is important because it frequently leads to American economic assistance. The power of recognition is less important now than in the 1900–1940 period, when Presidents used this authority to make and unmake Latin American governments.

The President shares with the Senate the right to enter into treaties with other countries. Treaties between nations are similar to contracts between persons, and they are an important feature of international relations. The President takes the initiative in treaty making, and the negotiations are conducted under his direction. However, the final product

"FIRST IN PEACE."    Air transportation makes it possible for the President
to join other chiefs of state in "summit conferences" in places distant from
the United States. Here President Ford meets with First Secretary Brezhnev
of the Soviet Union in Asian Russia to discuss strategic arms limitations.
*(Official Photograph, The White House, David Hume Kennerly)*

must be approved by a two-thirds majority of the Senate before it becomes law. One of the great tragedies of presidential history was the rejection of the treaty that created the League of Nations at the end of World War I. Woodrow Wilson had conceived the idea of an international organization that could settle disputes among nations, thus reducing the danger of war. The participation of the United States in the League became the President's foremost objective. But the Treaty of Versailles authorizing American membership in the League of Nations was rejected by the Senate, and Wilson died a broken-hearted man.

In recent years, Presidents frequently have bypassed the Senate by entering into executive agreements. These are understandings reached by heads of nations, and like treaties they have the force of law. A good example of an executive agreement was the arrangement that Franklin D. Roosevelt made with British Prime Minister Churchill before the United States entered World War II. Roosevelt agreed to put fifty American destroyers at the disposal of Great Britain in return for the right to use British military bases in the Caribbean and to construct new ones there.

Executive agreements have been opposed by many senators on the grounds that they allow a President to reach an understanding with another head of government that might be unacceptable to the Senate if put in the form of a treaty. Presidents have defended their use of executive agreements by pointing out that they greatly simplify the conduct of foreign policy. Moreover, when an agreement reached with another head of government requires an appropriation to carry it out, Congress must approve.

As director of foreign affairs, the President sometimes

states American policy in a formal, official manner. A good example is the Monroe Doctrine. This famous statement of the long-range Latin American policy of the United States was drawn up by John Quincy Adams, secretary of state in the Monroe administration, and made official by the President in 1823. Another notable statement of American foreign-policy objectives was the Fourteen Points outlined by President Woodrow Wilson as the proper basis for concluding peace at the end of World War I.

The President entrusts the day-by-day conduct of foreign affairs to the policy-making officials whom he names, subject to Senate approval. Ordinarily, the most important of these aides is the secretary of state. The secretary advises the President on the conduct of international relations and is the head of the department of state, or foreign office, of the United States. The secretary's most important assistants are appointed by the President, but the vast majority of the department's employees are career officers. They are specially trained for the conduct of foreign affairs, pass an examination that qualifies them for appointment, and generally remain with the department for many years.

Many of the career officers of the department of state work in Washington, while others are members of the foreign service and serve their country abroad. The most important foreign-service officers are the ambassadors who represent the United States in each nation that it recognizes. Ambassadors are appointed by the President with the approval of the Senate, and they may be recalled at any time by the Chief Executive. In the past, many ambassadors received their appointments because they contributed large sums of money to the candidate who won the presidential election.

This practice has been curtailed because of the recent restrictions on campaign contributions that were described in earlier chapters. However, members of the President's party who are wealthy enough to bear part of the expense of maintaining an embassy in a major nation have an edge in securing appointments as ambassadors. As the standards of the foreign service have been raised, an increasing number of ambassadors have been chosen from among the career officers who know the language of the country to which they are sent, and are familiar with its problems.

Presidents generally depend upon their secretaries of state for guidance, but several Presidents have made other officials their chief assistants in the conduct of foreign affairs. Recent Presidents have relied heavily on members of the National Security Council in developing foreign policy. Two wartime Presidents had unofficial advisers who exerted tremendous influence in the conduct of international affairs. Woodrow Wilson made Colonel House, whose title was honorary, his trusted adviser, and his personal representative to Allied leaders during World War I. House became an admired and envied figure because of the responsibilities that the President entrusted to him. In World War II, Harry Hopkins served as President Roosevelt's troubleshooter and confidant in the management of foreign affairs. In that capacity, Harry Hopkins became a well-known figure in the capitals of the world.

## MATTERS OF WAR AND PEACE

The President's role as commander in chief has been considered separately from his role as director of foreign affairs to simplify matters. Actually there is no boundary between war and peace in the modern world, as there is no boundary between foreign affairs and domestic affairs. Attention already has been called to the fact that the military establishment, which is geared for war, dominates the peacetime economy of the United States. As director of foreign affairs, the President administers the multibillion-dollar foreign-aid program of the United States. But economic aid has military objectives, quite apart from its being used to improve socio-economic conditions in developing nations. In theory at least, loans, gifts of food, the provision of technical advice, and the sale of industrial equipment all strengthen weak nations and keep them on the side of the United States in its world-wide struggle with the Communist powers.

The role of the President as commander in chief is difficult to distinguish from his role as director of foreign affairs for yet another reason. In playing each role, the President has the same objective: to maintain the position of the United States as the leading nation of the world. The President attempts to keep his country in first place through tactics developed with the advice of the secretary of state and other foreign-policy advisers. But when the President feels that the interests of the United States are threatened, he may change his role as chief diplomat for that of military chief. Peaceful efforts having failed, the President resorts to war. And at the end of war, it is the President who makes peace.

The interchangeable wartime and peacetime roles of the President were demonstrated at the time the atomic bomb was being developed. President Franklin Roosevelt ordered scientists and engineers to proceed with the project, which

"FIRST IN WAR." As commander in chief of the armed forces of the United States, the President is responsible for the maintenance, deployment, and strategy of the world's most formidable military establishment. Here President John F. Kennedy inspects a unit of the United States Navy. *(Official U.S. Navy Photograph, 1963)*

THE PRESIDENT AS WORLD LEADER. As the United States has grown in economic might, its political and military influence has increased to the point where the nation is regarded as the leader of the Free World. As director of foreign affairs, the President receives visiting heads of state and discusses high policy with them. Here President and Mrs. Eisenhower welcome Queen Elizabeth II of Great Britain and her consort, Prince Philip. (*Copyright by White House Historical Association, photograph by National Geographic Society*)

was considered necessary for ultimate victory over Hitler and his allies. At the same time, the President considered the peacetime uses of nuclear energy. At the President's command, the most terrible of all weapons would be used to end the most terrible of all wars. But at the conclusion of that war, nuclear power could provide the world with an unlimited supply of energy that could be used to abolish hunger, reduce poverty, and curb disease.

Today the President of the United States has power undreamed of by Polk, Lincoln, and Wilson. He is one of the heads of government who decides whether the people of the world will be destroyed by a final war or live in peace. For at any moment, and without consulting Congress, the President may decide that a threat to the security of the United States makes it necessary for him to use his ultimate power: to launch a nuclear attack on another nation simply by pressing buttons and giving telephoned commands. In other words, the President of the United States has the power to determine the ultimate fate of mankind.

# VIII

# CHECKMATING
# THE PRESIDENT

As the fateful hour approached, millions of Americans switched on their television sets and waited for the program to begin. No one doubted the importance of the approaching telecast because commentators had described it as one of the most significant events in the history of the republic. The telecast would have an impressive setting and a notable cast of characters. The issue to be decided affected the future of democratic government in the United States. And to make the televised proceedings even more dramatic, their outcome was uncertain.

The telecast of July 24, 1974, originated in the majestic hearing room of an office building of the House of Representatives. Because of the gravity of the occasion, Congress had relaxed its rule against televising its transactions. The cast of characters assembled in the hearing room that evening consisted of the full membership of the Judiciary Committee of the House of Representatives. However, the central role belonged to a figure who remained offstage—Richard M. Nixon, President of the United States.

After long investigation and debate, the House Judiciary Committee had met to decide whether the President's conduct of his office made him subject to impeachment. (Impeachment is a formal charge brought against a government official by the lower house of a legislature. The upper house of the legislature must then try the person who is accused of misusing the authority of his office. If found guilty, the official is removed.)

It was the duty of the Judiciary Committee to recommend what, if any, action the House of Representatives as a whole should take against the President. If the House voted to bring charges of official misconduct against the President, the Senate would have to try him. But the verdict of the House Judiciary Committee was unpredictable. It depended upon the interpretation that each member placed upon a provision of the Constitution—that a President may be impeached only on charges of "treason, bribery, or other high crimes and misdemeanors." The meaning of the first two words was clear, but what constituted a high crime or misdemeanor? Did those words fit the President's acts? Those were the questions in every mind. The issue was complicated by the fact that Richard Nixon was a Republican, while Democrats constituted a majority of the committee that was about to pass judgment on him.

Many Americans who watched the proceedings had simplified the problem in their minds. To them, the question was whether the most powerful ruler in the democratic world was accountable to the people who had placed him in office. Could Richard M. Nixon—who exercised awesome power as Chief Executive, chief legislator, party chieftain, director of foreign affairs, and commander in chief of the armed forces—could President Richard M. Nixon be checked by Congress, acting in the name of the people of the United States?

Some authorities on government believed that recent Presidents had upset the balance between executive and legislative power that the Founding Fathers had established. These experts spoke of the "imperial presidency," and regarded Congress as almost powerless to cope with a determined Chief Executive. President Nixon's commanding position seemed to support that view. He had been reelected by a landslide, carrying forty-nine of the fifty states in 1972. He had strong support from the business community and from agricultural interests. He had successfully maintained his right to reorganize the executive department so as to lessen congressional oversight. When Congress appropriated money for programs that it regarded as necessary, the President refused to spend the funds when he disapproved of their intended use. He had waged a ruthless war in Indochina, a war that Congress had not declared, and ordered the invasion of Cambodia, a neutral nation. In conducting his undeclared war, President Nixon frequently deceived Congress, and even more freqently deceived the general public.

The President's actions had antagonized a number of senators and representatives, and alarmed many civic leaders. However, the move to impeach Richard Nixon came about because of his less public activities. The burglary of the headquarters of the Democratic National Committee in the

Watergate complex in Washington in 1972 was a seemingly insignificant event that ultimately aroused the nation.

A routine police investigation connected the burglary to President Nixon's campaign organization. It was not long before investigative reporters for the *Washington Post* and other newspapers discovered that several of President Nixon's principal aides not only had been involved in the burglary, but also had been party to other illegal activities. Some of the President's advisers then began to admit their guilt and to implicate other members of the White House staff. The attorney general resigned under pressure when it became apparent that he was involved in the Watergate affair.

Several months elapsed before a Senate committee began its investigation of the Watergate break-in and its aftermath. The hearings revealed a pattern of wrongdoing in the White House. Illegal campaign funds had been accepted by the Committee to Reelect the President. The Federal Bureau of Investigation, the Central Intelligence Agency, and the Internal Revenue Service had been used to strike at the President's opponents and to further his own political goals. The President's aides had been involved in burglarizing the quarters of individuals and organizations opposed to his policies, in tapping their telephones, and in reading their mail. In the course of the Senate investigation, a member of the White House staff disclosed the fact that the President's conversations with his principal aides had been taped. It was those tapes that proved the President's undoing.

In the meantime, President Nixon had named a new attorney general and authorized him to appoint a special prosecutor to probe the Watergate affair. The special prosecutor promptly took legal action to secure the President's taped conversations, which were considered essential for the impending investigation. When it became apparent that the special prosecutor intended to get to the bottom of the Watergate affair, the President ordered his dismissal. The newly appointed attorney general resigned in protest. This caused what newspaper editors described as a fire storm of public protest. Thousands of angry citizens wrote their senators and representatives demanding the impeachment and removal of President Nixon.

In response to the outcry, the President agreed to hand over the tapes, and to appoint a new special prosecutor. But the position of the Chief Executive worsened by the day. A grand jury (a group of from sixteen to twenty-three persons chosen from voting lists to hear evidence of crime and to determine whether the facts submitted to it necessitate a trial) ordered seven of the President's principal aides to stand trial for their involvement in the Watergate break-in. The grand jurors indicated that they regarded the President himself as party to the wrongdoing, even though he was not indicted, or charged.

The President released some of the tapes, but refused to yield others. Finally a second special prosecutor who had been appointed took legal action to secure the tapes, and the Supreme Court agreed to hear the case. On July 24, 1974 —the day that the Judiciary Committee of the House of Representatives began its televised debate on impeachment —the Supreme Court ordered the President to release the tapes. The President agreed to comply.

After weeks of investigation, study, and discussion, members of the House Judiciary Committee assembled before the television cameras that July evening in 1974, either to charge the President with misconduct that warranted his impeachment, or to defend him before the people of the United States and to demand that the charges against him be dismissed.

The sincerity and the eloquence of the members of the House of Representatives who spoke that night and on the days that followed were impressive. Few who watched the proceedings doubted that each member of the committee had searched his conscience before he spoke.

Members of the House Judiciary Committee prepared to vote on the articles of impeachment that had been drafted as millions of their fellow citizens watched and listened. The bipartisan committee at length authorized three articles of impeachment. The first charged President Nixon with obstructing justice by attempting to prevent the lawful investigation of the Watergate break-in, and with "Making false or misleading public statements for the purpose of deceiving the people of the United States. . . ." The second article accused the President of violating the constitutional rights of citizens by using the tax-collection system for his political purposes, and by authorizing wiretapping and investigations unrelated to national security or law enforcement. The third article charged the President with refusing to respond to the committee's demands for information needed for its inquiry, thus substituting his judgment for that of investigators whom the Constitution had authorized to secure evidence needed for an independent inquiry.

Even before the vote, the leadership of the House of Representatives had concluded that a majority of the Judiciary Committee would recommend impeachment. Accordingly plans were made for debate on impeachment by the full membership of the House. And since Senate leaders felt certain that the House of Representatives would vote to impeach, they made ready for the President's trial.

But Richard M. Nixon was not impeached by the House nor tried by the Senate. On Monday, August 5, 1974, the President admitted that he had halted the investigation of the Watergate break-in, and that he had kept the evidence of that fact from his lawyers and his supporters. Three days later, when his impeachment by the House of Representatives and his conviction by the Senate appeared inevitable, Richard M. Nixon became the first President of the United States to resign from office.

## CONGRESS VERSUS PRESIDENT

Impeachment is the most dramatic and the most drastic method of curbing the power of the President. The framers of the Constitution made impeachment a difficult undertaking by limiting the charges that can be brought against the Chief Executive by the House of Representatives. And by having the Senate try the President after the House has impeached him, the Founding Fathers provided considerable protection for a Chief Executive.

Only one President—Andrew Johnson—has ever been impeached. President Johnson was tried by the Senate in 1868, with the Chief Justice of the United States presiding. He escaped conviction by one vote. Historians generally agree that President Johnson was impeached only because his Reconstruction policy had antagonized the Radical Republicans, who dominated the House of Representatives. His acquittal is now regarded as a very important event in presi-

THE PRESIDENT ON THE DEFENSIVE. Congress acts as a check on the President when it investigates any aspect of the executive branch of government. In this photograph, President Ford appears before the Judiciary Committee of the House of Representatives to explain why he pardoned his predecessor, Richard M. Nixon, after that President resigned before he could be impeached. *(Courtesy of A. Dev O'Neill, photographer to the Congress of the United States)*

dential history. Had Congress succeeded in removing Johnson from office for purely political reasons, the Presidency might have been brought under the domination of the legislative branch of government. This would have damaged the system of checks and balances outlined in the Constitution.

Although the Founding Fathers made impeachment difficult, they provided several other devices for keeping the President in his proper constitutional place. By establishing a four-year term of office, the framers of the Constitution enabled the voting public to pass judgment on Presidents at stated intervals. George Washington established a precedent when he refused to consider a third term, and until the administration of Franklin D. Roosevelt, Presidents followed the example set by the first Chief Executive. Roosevelt's four terms established a record that will not be broken, because with the adoption of the Twenty-second Amendment in 1951, the maximum time a President may hold office is two full terms, plus less than half of an unexpired term.

The principal checks on presidential power are exercised by Congress. Two of these curbs have already been noted: removal from office after impeachment and conviction, and investigation of the executive department. The Watergate investigations have been mentioned. During the Ford administration, both the Senate and the House of Representatives focused their attention on the Federal Bureau of Investigation and the Central Intelligence Agency. Each house of Congress pursued its investigation despite presidential opposition. As a result of these inquiries, Congress imposed restraints on the two powerful agencies that operate under the direction of the President.

As noted in Chapter VI, the President is the chief legislator because he proposes a great number of laws and tries to have them enacted. But even though an aggressive President has many methods of influencing Congress to do his bidding, still Congress has the final say. Laws that the President wants must be passed by Congress. And measures that the President opposes become the law of the land when Congress overrides his veto by a two-thirds majority.

As we have seen, the national budget is drawn up under the President's direction, and he oversees all expenditures. But the money that the President spends must be appropriated by Congress, and this control over the purse strings provides Congress with the means to hold a President in check. By denying a President the money that he requests, Congress may force him to alter his plans or abandon them. To emphasize its ultimate control over the finances of the national government, Congress recently established a budget office of its own. Experts in the Congressional Budget Office study the estimates submitted by the President and then provide senators and representatives with an analysis of the proposals. This information enables Congress to decide whether to accept, modify, or reject the President's requests.

Congress not only determines the amount of money that a President may spend, but it also can stipulate the manner in which the funds are to be used. Moreover Congress creates agencies within the executive department, outlines their responsibilities, and lays down the qualifications of their employees. Congress may go further in exercising its power to check the President. It may place restrictions on the use of executive authority. For example, in 1973 Congress overrode a Nixon veto and enacted legislation that limits a President's authority to wage war on his own initiative.

The measure requires the President to report to Congress within forty-eight hours any commitment of troops to foreign hostilities, along with an explanation of the circumstances, the authority for his action, and the expected scope of the military operation. The law requires the President to end hostilities within sixty days unless Congress has declared war or authorized the commitment of military forces. After the stated period has elapsed, Congress can force an immediate withdrawal of military forces by passing a concurrent resolution, which is not subject to veto. In short, Congress reasserted its authority in the field of foreign affairs.

## BYPASSING THE PRESIDENT

Congress may curb presidential power by yet another method. It may draw up a constitutional amendment, approve it by a two-thirds majority in both houses, and submit it to the states for ratification. Proposed amendments do not require presidential approval, and if adopted by three quarters of the states, they become part of the Constitution. In other words, presidential power may be curbed by altering the Constitution itself. A good example is the Twenty-second Amendment, which limits the President's tenure of office to two full terms. Harry Truman was President when this amendment was proposed, and he strongly objected to it. Congress, however, submitted the amendment to the states, despite the President's opposition, and it was ratified.

To this point the term *Congress* has been used in describing restraints on presidential power that are exercised jointly by the Senate and the House of Representatives. The Constitution gives to the Senate alone two other important curbs on the President. One is the provision that treaties must be approved by a two-thirds majority in the Senate. Ordinarily the Senate follows the lead of the President in treaty-making, but it reserves the right to insist on modification of the treaty submitted by the President, and as noted earlier, it may reject outright a treaty that the President has negotiated.

The Constitution also provides that the Senate must confirm the appointment of cabinet members, federal judges, ambassadors, and certain other important officials. Normally the Senate approves presidential appointments without question. On occasion, however, the Senate rejects a presidential nominee, thus forcing him to offer another candidate. President Nixon had a bitter quarrel with the Senate in 1969–1970 when it rejected first one and then another of his nominees to fill a vacancy on the Supreme Court. It was only on the third try that the Senate confirmed the President's choice.

To summarize, the Founding Fathers provided Congress with effective means to curb an aggressive President. But possessing authority is quite different from possessing the ability and the will to exercise that authority. Congress rarely closes ranks and faces the President with a united front.

Through the years, a congressional brake on presidential power has developed more or less apart from the Constitution. This unofficial check evolved as the standing, or permanent, committees of the Senate and the House of Representatives assumed more and more control over congressional affairs. The chairmen of these committees now exercise so much authority that they sometimes are referred to as "the lords proprietor of Congress."

Seniority is the chief factor in the choice of committee chairmen, which means that a senator or representative who is reelected time and time again may become a key figure in government. Presidents come and go, but some members of Congress seem to go on forever, having been returned to office for thirty, forty, or even fifty years. Committee chairmen not only know the workings of Congress to perfection, but through long experience they have learned how to deal with the White House. Moreover, they frequently have ties with important business and labor leaders who can bring pressure to bear on the President. In addition, committee chairmen are often on friendly terms with the heads of agencies and commissions within the executive department— officials who are responsible for carrying out the President's directives. Committee chairmen with such connections are in a position to challenge the President by using their influence with officials of executive departments to block presidential plans.

When compared with Congress, the Supreme Court is a minor brake on executive power. In fact, Clinton Rossiter, a leading authority on the Presidency, once remarked that for all practical purposes, the President may act as if the Supreme Court does not exist. For one thing, the Supreme Court generally has refused to consider what it regards as purely political disputes. The Court also has shown a tendency to avoid passing judgment on challenged acts of the President until the controversy has ceased to arouse great emotion. For example, a number of violations of civil rights that occurred during the Lincoln administration were not reviewed by the Supreme Court until after Lincoln was dead and the Civil War was over.

Some historians have observed that at the outset of that war, President Lincoln disregarded the Supreme Court's challenge to his authority to suppress civil rights. A notable example occurred in 1861 as a result of Lincoln's suspension of the writ of habeas corpus in certain parts of the Union. (As noted earlier, the writ of habeas corpus, long considered a basic civil rights guarantee, is a court order that requires officers making an arrest to bring their prisoner before a judge, who decides whether the detained person should be released or be held for further investigation.) Chief Justice Taney declared that Lincoln's suspension of habeas corpus was unconstitutional, and he demanded the release of a prisoner detained under the President's order. Lincoln ignored the Chief Justice's demand. Having been reminded of their inability to force compliance with their rulings, Supreme Court justices thereafter avoided passing judgment on the President's acts until the war ended.

More recently, the Supreme Court has challenged the President on several occasions, in each instance when it was conscious of wide public support. A good example of "Court versus President" occurred in 1952, when President Truman ordered his secretary of commerce to take over the operation of the nation's steel mills in order to avoid a strike. The President sent a message to Congress explaining that the steel industry was essential to the war effort in Korea, and that a work stoppage would endanger national security. Truman also made a nationwide radio address in which he called on the American people to support his action. The

President received little backing in Congress, and far less than he had expected from the general public. Business leaders, newspaper editors, and other influential citizens denounced the President for seizing private property.

The steel companies brought suit against the secretary of commerce, and the case (*Youngstown Sheet & Tube Company* v. *Sawyer*) came before the Supreme Court in short order. In a 6 to 3 decision, the High Court ruled against the President and ordered him to return the steel mills to their owners. The President promptly complied with the order. (Reference already has been made to a more recent Supreme Court judgment against the President. This was in 1974, when the Supreme Court ordered President Nixon to surrender the tapes that recorded his conversations bearing on the Watergate break-in to the special prosecutor who needed them for an investigation authorized by the Constitution.)

## BUILT-IN RESTRAINTS ON THE PRESIDENT

Some of the most effective restraints on presidential authority are exercised by members of the executive department itself. In fact, officials appointed by the President may consciously or unconsciously thwart his plans. The President has more than 2,500,000 subordinates in the civilian agencies of the executive department. The President's directives are carried out by these members of the federal bureaucracy, and the effectiveness of his administration depends not only upon the ability of his subordinates but also upon their willingness to comply with his orders. From time to time, the President dismisses one of his high-ranking subordinates who challenges or merely fails to comply with an executive order. A notable example occurred during the Korean War when President Truman relieved the famous and highly popular General Douglas MacArthur of his position as commander of American forces in the field. MacArthur publicly differed with his commander in chief as to strategy, and as a consequence was dismissed.

Presidents have had less difficulty in dealing with the open opposition of a high-ranking subordinate than in dealing with the silent opposition of less important members of the federal bureaucracy. Opposition to executive policy may lead one of the Chief Executive's subordinates to "leak" information that will damage the President, particularly when the information falls into the hands of hostile newspaper editors or television commentators. For instance, President Nixon's conduct of the war in Indochina was hampered by the publication of the Pentagon Papers, secret documents detailing American involvement in southeastern Asia that had been taken from the files of the Defense Department by Daniel Ellsberg, a former adviser, and given to *The New York Times.*

The President's subordinates sometimes undermine his authority by ignoring orders. This was made clear during the missile crisis of 1962, when President Kennedy demanded that the Russians withdraw the nuclear weapons that they were installing in Cuba. The Soviet leader countered by demanding that the United States remove its missiles from Turkey. The Russian response reminded President Kennedy that eighteen months previously he had ordered the removal of American missiles from Turkey in order to reduce international tension. The President's fateful negotiations with Soviet authorities had been jeopardized by a subordinate's failure to obey orders.

Generally speaking, the brakes on presidential authority that federal bureaucrats exercise are not as dramatic as the examples just cited. More often than not, it is inefficiency or indifference that acts as a curb. The President may issue a directive to his chief assistants, and they may pass the order down the line. Ultimately civil servants completely unknown to the President execute his policy. In this respect, the President is at the mercy of the lower ranks of the executive department. President Truman had this in mind when he commented on the plight of his successor, Dwight D. Eisenhower. Truman predicted that the former general would issue directives, thinking that they would be executed with the speed that he had become accustomed to in the army. "Poor Ike," President Truman said, "he will give an order and sit there waiting for it to be carried out. And nothing will happen."

## THE ROLE OF TELEVISION AND THE PRESS

The restraints on presidential power so far described operate within the framework of government. Now attention shifts to nongovernmental checks on the President, such as the press, television, and public-opinion polls.

George Washington was the subject of much attention in the newspapers of his day. Despite the first President's prestige and his popularity, he was not spared from attack. In letters that Washington wrote to trusted friends, he acknowledged that his conduct was influenced by the views that newspaper editors and cartoonists had of him. More often than not, it was adverse criticism that Washington alluded to; hostile editors seemed to carry more weight than those who supported him. From Washington's time to the present, Presidents have regarded newspapermen as desirable allies and formidable opponents.

Before radio and television became the chief sources of public information, the press exerted a profound influence throughout the nation. Horace Greeley and other well-known editors had a wide following, and when they addressed their readers, even Presidents listened with respect. William Mc-Kinley is sometimes mentioned as a President who changed an important policy because of pressure engendered by the press. President McKinley believed that war with Spain could be avoided, despite that country's harsh treatment of its rebellious colonists, the Cubans. But in 1898, the most aggressive editors of the day, William Randolph Hearst and Joseph Pulitzer, used the columns of their newspapers to create a popular clamor for American intervention in Cuba. Finally President McKinley yielded to pressure and asked Congress to declare war on Spain.

Newspapers and magazines have played a leading part in exposing the misdeeds of Presidents. The widespread graft that characterized the Grant administration was brought to public attention by enterprising reporters; and cartoonists, such as Thomas Nast, did not spare the President himself. In calling attention to President Grant's inability to control his corrupt subordinates, newspapers furthered the reform movement, and hastened the adoption of civil service at the national level.

Attention has already been directed to the role of congressional committees in laying bare the illegal practices of President Nixon and the principal members of his staff. But the "sleuthing" of the investigative reporters of the *Wash-*

*ington Post, Los Angeles Times,* and several other newspapers were of equal importance in acquainting the
American people with the misdeeds of the President and the
Vice-President whom they elected in 1972. Many political
scientists regard the newspaper articles, books, and films
that described the Watergate scandal as having had a long-
lasting effect on the Presidency. Such accounts exposed the
inner workings of the executive department, described the
way in which the power of government may be misused, and
made clear the need for additional checks on presidential
authority. As a result of the exposure of presidential wrongdoing, American voters were made more critical of future
candidates for office.

In stressing the role of newspaper editors, reporters, and
columnists in checking presidential authority, the equally
important role of televised political events should not be
overlooked. It was television that brought the Senate Watergate investigation into millions of homes, forcing citizens
to consider ways of preventing a repetition of the criminal
acts that they had heard described in such detail. And it
was television that enabled the American people to judge
the President for themselves, having listened to the charges
brought against him by the House Judiciary Comittee.

To this description of television as a check on executive
authority must be added the effect of the nightly analyses
of the Presidency given by astute commentators during the
constitutional crisis of 1974. A number of these news
analysts jarred the thinking of their listeners, and made
them understand that the Watergate break-in was only the
surface detail of a deep-seated problem. The commentators
reminded Americans that the misuse of presidential power

is an old story. And while condemning Nixon, the analysts pointed out that his predecessors, Kennedy and Johnson, had instituted several practices for which he was censured.

Another nongovernmental check on presidential authority is the public-opinion poll. Presidents are now rated as to their standing with the American people. A President who occupies a high position on the approval scale knows that his conduct of office is acceptable to the majority of citizens. A low position on the approval scale indicates that the President is unpopular because of policies that he is pursuing.

Some public-opinion polls rate Presidents at stated intervals, while others conduct special surveys after a controversial act—such as a decision to reduce the flow of arms to Israel, or to reach an understanding with the People's Republic of China. In theory at least, public-opinion polls act as a check on the President because he does not wish to continue a policy that the general public opposes, particularly if he is seeking reelection.

## THE PEOPLE AND THEIR PRESIDENT

In this chapter, numerous restraints on presidential authority have been considered. Particular stress has been placed on the way in which Congress reasserted its authority after the forced resignation of President Nixon. But no thoughtful American will conclude that the delicate balance in government that the Founding Fathers contrived has been attained, and that means have been found to keep future Presidents from trespassing on the rights of Congress and from threatening the rights of the people. As a reaction to the Watergate scandal, the Presidency came to be regarded

PUTTING PRESSURE ON THE PRESIDENT. The White House attracts concerned individuals, as well as massive crowds, who wish to influence public policy by bringing pressure to bear on the President. Here a suffragette maintains a vigil at the White House gates in an effort to rally support for the Nineteenth Amendment, which gave women the right to vote. *(Copyright by White House Historical Association, photograph by National Geographic Society)*

with suspicion by many Americans. But when a future crisis develops at home or abroad, citizens undoubtedly will turn to the President and welcome his prompt, bold action. Then the White House will again be in the ascendancy, and the Capitol will lose ground. At least this is the view held by a number of authorities on American government. Such experts point out that through the years, "strong" Presidents have expanded executive authority at the expense of Congress. But aggressive Presidents usually have been followed by Chief Executives who show little interest in adding to the powers of their office. These less forceful Presidents have been content to have Congress exercise at least an equal voice in government.

The simplicity of this view of the Presidency makes it appealing. It is also reassuring to believe that the operation of the checks-and-balance system is automatic. But the constitutional crisis created by the Watergate break-in seems to show that the American people possibly escaped some form of tyranny only because a small number of alert citizens discovered hidden, evil forces and exposed them. The episode was a reminder that the most effective check on the President of the United States is a well-informed citizenry that is determined to remain free from all forms of oppression.

# IX

# PRESIDENTS
# ON PARADE

A crowd had gathered at the foot of Mount Rushmore in the Black Hills of South Dakota. The airplanes that circled overhead attracted attention, but the real point of interest was the enormous American flag suspended from the mountain peak. Underneath that red, white, and blue covering was the attraction that had drawn people from across the nation to a wild, remote site. While the crowd watched, riflemen took position. They fired a salute, and the great flag was withdrawn. All eyes focused on the cliff, where the face of George Washington had been carved from the living rock. The program notes explained that the likeness of the first President measured 60 feet from chin to forehead, which made it twice as tall as the head of the famous Sphinx in Egypt.

The heroic image of George Washington was part of a

project authorized by Congress in 1925 and finally completed in 1941. After the likeness of the first President was completed, the heads of Jefferson, Lincoln, and Theodore Roosevelt were carved on the granite cliff by Gutzon Borglum, a sculptor noted for his gigantic statues. Today the stupendous grouping is designated as the Shrine of Democracy, and the site is known as the Mount Rushmore National Memorial. Of the millions of Americans who have seen the monument, many believe that Washington, Jefferson, Lincoln, and Theodore Roosevelt were honored because they were officially chosen as the greatest Presidents of the United States. Actually the four Presidents represent the preferences of the sculptor himself. When he proposed to carve the likenesses of Washington and Lincoln on the face of the mountain, no one questioned his choice. There was little criticism of his decision to place Jefferson alongside Washington and Lincoln. It was his fourth choice that produced vigorous opposition. But Borglum went ahead with his sculpture, despite protests that Theodore Roosevelt was not entitled to be in such exalted company.

## RANKING THE PRESIDENTS

The Presidents of the United States had been rated many times before Borglum made his famous choice. Since the beginning of the republic, Americans have shown their preference by honoring some Presidents and ignoring others. For example, Washington's birthday was widely celebrated as a holiday even while he lived. The nation's capital, a state, thirty-one counties, and innumerable towns, colleges, and parks have been named for the first President. Both

A PRESIDENTIAL WEDDING.    The activities of the President and his family always have been of great interest to the American people, and White House functions have influenced social customs from the Washington administration onward. This illustration depicts the marriage of President Grover Cleveland with Frances Folsom in the White House, 1886. *(From* Frank Leslie's Illustrated Newspaper, *reproduced from the collection of the Library of Congress)*

Jefferson and Lincoln have been honored by having a state capital named after them, along with numerous counties, highways, and institutions of higher learning. Visitors to the national capital might conclude that Washington, Lincoln, and Jefferson are considered the three greatest Presidents because their memorial monuments are the most impressive in a city of splendid buildings.

Rating the Presidents of the United States by any of the devices so far mentioned is a somewhat haphazard way of making comparisons. Accordingly historians and political scientists have created rating systems of their own. The most notable of these was devised by Arthur Schlesinger, Sr., a professor of American history at Harvard University. In 1948 and again in 1962, Schlesinger asked seventy-five leading historians to rate the Presidents of the United States on the basis of their accomplishments in office. The experts were to classify the Presidents under five headings: great, near great, average, below average, or failure. The historians who were polled rated Lincoln, Washington, Franklin D. Roosevelt, Wilson, and Jefferson as great. They classified Jackson, Theodore Roosevelt, Polk, Truman, John Adams, and Cleveland as near great. Taylor, Tyler, Fillmore, Coolidge, Pierce, and Buchanan were rated below average, while Grant and Harding were classified as failures. The remaining Presidents were rated as average.

The Schlesinger polls attracted wide attention, but a number of authorities on American history and government warned against placing too much faith in any system for rating Presidents. In his book, *Presidential Greatness*, Thomas A. Bailey of Stanford University pointed out that most historians are liberal in their politics, and tend to be

Democrats by party membership. When they rate the Presidents, historians tend to regard as successful those who have acted boldly, and who have extended executive authority. They have small use for Presidents who were not aggressive. In short, Bailey argued that the background and political views of the expert who ranks the Presidents influences the ratings that he gives.

The year in which Presidents are appraised also affects the way they are ranked. James Bryce, a leading British authority on government, wrote *The American Commonwealth*, which was published in 1888, and it has remained a foremost study of the political system of the United States. The most controversial chapter in Bryce's work was "Why Great Men Are Not Chosen President." The English writer first declared that the Presidency is the greatest office in the world that a man may attain by his own merits, with the possible exception of the Papacy. Bryce then gave several reasons why great Americans were rarely elected President, among them the fact that in the United States men of ability were more likely to be drawn into business than into politics. Bryce also felt that the method of selecting presidential candidates did not produce Chief Executives of distinction, and that American voters were willing to accept mediocrity in the Presidency. In the most quoted chapter of his book, Bryce evaluated the Presidents. The British expert's opinion, made many years ago, is of interest today because he gave a favorable rating to Grant, who is now regarded as having been a very weak President, and a low rating to Polk, who is now highly regarded by students of the Presidency.

Fifty years after Bryce appraised the Presidents, Harold

Laski, another British authority on American government, challenged the ideas that his countryman had popularized. Laski argued that the United States had by that time had as many great Presidents as Great Britain had great Prime Ministers in the same period. The British authority then named seven Presidents whom he considered great: Washington, Jefferson, Jackson, Lincoln, Theodore Roosevelt, Wilson, and Franklin D. Roosevelt.

The changes in presidential ratings that the passage of time may bring about were acknowledged by Emmet John Hughes, once an adviser of President Eisenhower. In his book, *The Living Presidency,* Hughes noted that Woodrow Wilson was hailed as the champion of human rights on the national and world stage while he served as President. At the end of World War I, there was a reaction to American involvement in world affairs, and the nation became isolationist in sentiment. During that period, Woodrow Wilson was downgraded by many Americans as a clumsy idealist. But once the United States became involved in World War II, Wilson was again made into something of a saintly prophet. In short, the changing appraisals of Wilson serve as a reminder that the standards by which Presidents are judged change from one period to another.

Some authorities on government believe that it is impossible to arrive at an objective, impartial rating of the Presidents for yet another reason. The historians and political scientists who make the attempt cannot judge the President solely on the basis of his conduct in executive office. They cannot avoid considering what he accomplished before he became President and what he achieved afterward. James Madison, for example, was called "the Father of

THE PRESIDENT ON STAGE.    Early Presidents made exhausting tours by
stage coach in order to maintain contact with the American people. Travel
by railroad and airplane enabled later Presidents to appear before vast
numbers of their countrymen within a brief period of time. Today the
President may be seen and heard by virtually every person in the United
States when he appears on television. Here President Ford conducts a
televised press conference in the rose garden of the White House. *(Copyright
by White House Historical Association, photograph by National Geographic
Society)*

the Constitution," a title that emphasizes his profound influence on American government. When Madison is rated as a President, are his notable accomplishments before he entered the White House considered or only his record as President?

Thomas Jefferson is classified as "great" on almost all ratings of the Presidents of the United States. But when Jefferson is appraised, is it as author of the Declaration of Independence and other documents of fundamental importance, or as Chief Executive? In this instance, some political scientists say that Jefferson can hardly be regarded as a successful President because his foreign policy was a near disaster. As author and diplomat, Jefferson was outstanding prior to his election as President, and those accomplishments influence the ratings given by historians. On the other hand, it is John Quincy Adams's record *after* leaving the Presidency that impresses some historians. They are influenced by his career in the House of Representatives, where "Old Man Eloquent" became one of the nation's foremost opponents of slavery.

## YARDSTICKS AND THEIR WORTH

Rating the Presidents is much more than an interesting game that historians play, more than the basis for hot debate between Democrats and Republicans. Ranking the Chief Executives provides instruction not only for would-be occupants of the White House, but also for the voting public, which in the final analysis determines the quality of the Presidents. The rating systems devised by historians and political scientists have their critics, but they do establish a basis of comparison—a yardstick on which Presidents can be measured. In setting standards for the conduct of the presidential office, experts on government identify characteristics that have made some Presidents "great" and some Presidents "failures." At the same time, the rating scales call attention to the circumstances that have favored presidential greatness and conditions that have led to failure.

Americans who aspire to be President invariably study the careers of "great" Presidents and use them as models. Presidential hopefuls discover common characteristics in the "great" Presidents and similarities in the way they came to power. With the exception of George Washington, all of the "great" and "near great" Presidents fought hard for high office. In fact, all the highly rated Presidents fought hard for the Presidency itself, except for Harry Truman, who inherited the office upon the death of Franklin D. Roosevelt. (Truman fought hard for reelection, however.) Of the men who were more or less handed the presidential nomination on a silver platter because they were military heroes (Harrison, Taylor, Grant, and Eisenhower), none is now ranked as "great" or "near great."

Presidents who have had little or no experience in elective office prior to becoming Chief Executive are not found in the "great" or "near great" classification. The most notable example is Herbert Hoover, who was an outstanding success as an appointed official, but who is generally regarded as having been an unsuccessful President. Hoover's career seems to bear out comments on the Presidency made by one of Franklin D. Roosevelt's advisers, David Lilienthal. After saying that the best preparation for the Presidency is the trial of running for and holding *elective* office, Lilienthal added that the worst preparation is strictly managerial or business experience.

Holding elective office for a long period permits the future Chief Executive to develop the qualities displayed by all "great" Presidents. Richard E. Neustadt, whose book *Presidential Power* is said to have influenced several Presidents, beginning with John F. Kennedy, has called attention to several characteristics that are common to successful Presidents. Theodore Roosevelt, Woodrow Wilson, and other Presidents likewise have noted traits that make for successful Chief Executives. The "great" Presidents, we are told, not only have complete confidence in themselves, but they also have a sense of direction. They know what power is, and they know how to wield it. "Great" Presidents have all been astute politicians, and all have displayed a certain toughness. Jimmy Carter, when campaigning for the Presidency in 1976, said that to be successful, a President must be strong and aggressive.

Carter's opinion is supported by the records of the "great" and "near great" Presidents. The strong Presidents all gave battle to Congress or the federal courts and sometimes to both branches. Jefferson brought about the impeachment (but not the removal) of a Supreme Court justice whom he found objectionable, and quarreled with Chief Justice Marshall as long as he was President. Franklin Roosevelt was so aroused by the Supreme Court's opposition to New Deal legislation that he made an unsuccessful attempt to "pack" the high court with justices more to his liking. All the strong Presidents have struggled with Congress, and some of those battles have been described in earlier chapters. President

Truman dramatized his bout with Congress by calling it into special session in order to demonstrate what he regarded as its shortcomings. In the ensuing presidential campaign, Truman made the "do-nothing" Congress a major issue.

In one sense, "great" Presidents have achieved that rank because they have struggled with Congress, and in so doing have extended executive power. As one reviews the history of the Presidency, he observes that when a strong President follows a weak Chief Executive, the strong President reaches back to his nearest aggressive predecessor and builds from that point on. In other words, strong Presidents jealously preserve what previous Chief Executives have achieved, and regard a further development of presidential authority as their obligation.

But in another sense, "great" Presidents have achieved that rank primarily because of the age in which they lived. Each "great" President has served in time of national crisis, and while each has responded vigorously to the threat, the influence of the times on the man is apparent. Abraham Lincoln, who had been a rather obscure representative from Illinois, was so challenged by the impending disintegration of the Union that he became what the historian Samuel Eliot Morison called a "dictator from the standpoint of American constitutional law." Franklin Roosevelt came to office as the nation faced economic collapse, and having used drastic means to avert catastrophe, he then led the nation through a global war. But perhaps the best example of the effect of crisis in developing presidential character was Harry Truman, considered by many Americans as a second-rate senator who inherited the Presidency just as some of the most momentous decisions in the history of the republic had to be made. The response of the "Little Man from Missouri" to the challenge that suddenly faced him has earned him the high rank that many leading Americans now accord him. (For example, as they campaigned for the Presidency in 1976, both Republican Gerald Ford and Democrat Jimmy Carter paid tribute to Harry Truman and acknowledged their debt to him.)

## PRESIDENTS OF THE FUTURE

Americans can learn a great deal by comparing the records of their Chief Executives. Presidential aspirants may discover ways of gaining the prize they seek, and once in office may employ strategies that brought success to an earlier Chief Executive, and avoid mistakes that ruined the career of another. Citizens who know something of presidential records are in a better position to select the nominee of their party when they vote in a primary, and to choose wisely between candidates when they vote in a general election. As voters learn about the qualities of the more distinguished Presidents of the past, they are likely to reject candidates who do not promise well.

But it is not enough for the nation to have many men and women who may become "great" Presidents if placed in office. And it is not enough to have well-informed citizens who are capable of choosing qualified Presidents. Great Americans must be encouraged to offer themselves as candidates, and voters must be permitted to choose freely from a wide field of presidential hopefuls. Moreover means must be found to persuade the millions of qualified Americans who neglect to vote to go to the polls and help select the President who exercises such vast influence over their lives.

In reviewing the history of the Presidency, one finds some reason to believe that the caliber of the Presidents of the United States has improved since James Bryce wrote his famous work. Certainly the method of choosing presidential candidates has become more democratic through the years, and presidential elections have become more open as well. In the first years of the republic, presidential candidates were chosen by the caucus method. In other words, a small group of political leaders chose the candidate of their party. It became the practice for senators and representatives belonging to each party to choose its presidential candidate. Selecting presidential candidates by the caucus method came in for much criticism. For one thing, it gave the legislative branch of government considerable influence over the executive branch. For another, the system was somewhat secret in operation, which made it possible for a few people to retain their control over nominations.

A new method of choosing presidential candidates developed during what has been called the "Second American Revolution"—the Jacksonian era when the hold over the national government that Easterners had long exercised was successfully challenged by leaders from the West. Political parties then discarded the caucus method of choosing presidential candidates and set up conventions for that purpose. As noted in Chapter IV, presidential nominating conventions allow wide participation in the choice of party candidates. But many civic leaders regarded nominating conventions as being unduly influenced by party bosses, whose control over local and state political machines placed them in command of large blocs of delegates who voted as they were told. To bring an end to this undemocratic system, Governor Robert La Follette of Wisconsin and other reformers proposed to choose presidential and vice-presidential candidates by means of elections where all party members could vote for the nominees of their choice. Having selected candidates at party, or primary, elections in the spring or summer, voters would then choose the President at the general election in the fall.

Between 1900 and World War I, twenty-six states enacted presidential primary laws. Then a reaction set in, and some states went back to the old system of choosing delegates to the presidential conventions. But after World War II, presidential primaries became part of a new reform movement. By the time the 1976 presidential campaign began, thirty states provided for presidential primary elections. As noted in Chapter IV, presidential primaries vary from state to state, not only as to when they are held but also in their operation. However, the purpose of all presidential primaries is the same: to allow the ordinary voter to influence the selection of presidential candidates.

Presidential primaries permit little-known candidates to make themselves national figures, and to force party leaders to consider them as nominees. Both John F. Kennedy (1960) and Jimmy Carter (1976) are examples of candidates who used the primaries to prove their popularity with voters, thus overcoming the opposition of a number of powerful party leaders. On the other hand, party leaders on several occasions have ignored the fine showing made by candidates in presidential primaries. In 1952, for example, the Democratic convention nominated Governor Adlai Stevenson of Illinois, who had not entered the presidential primaries, instead of Senator Estes Kefauver of Tennessee, who had won twelve of the fourteen presidential preference primaries that he entered.

## WHY A GREAT MAN
## MAY NOT BE CHOSEN PRESIDENT

Presidential candidates are now chosen more democratically than they were at the beginning of the republic. Highly qualified but relatively unknown men and women may enter primaries and quickly call attention to themselves. Presidential candidates are able to campaign widely because they receive financial support from the federal government. These subsidies permit the use of television, a medium that allows the candidate to lay his case before voters in all parts of the nation.

Thanks to another new development in American political life—the public-opinion poll—a presidential candidate may strengthen his hand with the party leaders who dominate the national conventions. This fact was borne out by a study recently made by William R. Keech, a research associate at the Brookings Institution in Washington. In analyzing election returns since 1936, Keech found that the candidate who leads the Gallup Poll of the rank-and-file members of his own party just before the start of the presidential primaries is likely to win at the national convention. The study seems to indicate that even though party leaders would prefer to name a candidate entirely of their own choosing, they yield to the wishes of the voting public.

THE EVER-CHANGING WHITE HOUSE. Alterations made in the Executive Mansion through the years typify the changing character of the Presidency itself. The White House was first occupied by John Adams, the second President, and his wife, Abigail. The mansion was rebuilt after being burned by British soldiers in the War of 1812. The historic structure has been renovated many times, and the interior was completely rebuilt during the Truman Administration. Changes in decoration and furnishings are made as one President succeeds another. (From Harper's Weekly, 1877, reproduced from the collection of the New York Public Library)

On the other hand, some critics believe that public-opinion polls exert a harmful influence in American politics. For one thing, they encourage voters to "jump on the band-wagon"—to follow the crowd—to be influenced more by the popularity of a candidate than by his real worth. Thus while public opinion polls may lessen the influence of party bosses in naming presidential candidates, those same polls give undue support to candidates who are more personable than qualified.

Great men now have more opportunity to be elected President than they had in the past. But this statement tends to be true only if the would-be President is either a Republican or a Democrat. If the highly qualified candidate belongs to a third party, the system for choosing Presidents discriminates against him. For one thing, all the electoral votes of each state are awarded to the candidate that receives the greatest number of popular votes. Even if a candidate carries a state by a single vote, he captures all the electoral votes of that state (with the exception of Maine, as noted in Chapter IV). This "winner-takes-all" system of allocating electoral votes almost always shuts out the candidate of a third party. Everyone likes a winner, and so the average American does not want to risk voting for a third-party candidate, even if he thinks that candidate is more qualified to serve as President.

Since they are regarded as certain losers, the candidates of third parties have difficulty in raising money to begin their campaigns for the Presidency. And since federal funds for campaigning in primary elections are awarded on a matching basis, candidates who cannot raise money do not receive subsidies. At a time when airplanes and television are essential to presidential campaigning, the third-party candidate is at a great disadvantage. He has little money to spend on these expensive campaign aids, while the candidates of major parties are able to charter planes and to buy television time.

A third party may nominate an outstanding person as its presidential candidate, but few voters will see or hear the nominee because he is financially disadvantaged. In the opinion of a number of political scientists, this is an unfortunate fact. The candidates of third parties have made important contributions to American life. In the 1840s, candidates of the Liberty party warned the American people that slavery threatened to disrupt the Union. In the 1870s and 1880s, the presidential nominees of the Greenback party called attention to the plight of farmers and urban workers. Candidates of the Prohibition party led the drive that resulted in the adoption of the Eighteenth Amendment, which banned the manufacture, sale, or transportation of intoxicating liquors. Nominees of the People's party (Populist) in 1896 and 1900, and of the Progressive party in 1924 called for governmental curbs on Big Business and also campaigned for other reforms. Between them, Eugene Debs and Norman Thomas ran eleven times as the presidential candidate of the Socialist party in the years between 1900 and 1948. (Debs was the only presidential candidate who ever campaigned from jail. In 1920, while he was still in prison because of his opposition to American participation in World War I, Debs polled almost 1,000,000 votes.)

These Socialist presidential candidates affected the thinking of countless Americans as they called attention to the weaknesses of the capitalist system. Many of the proposals made by Debs and Thomas later became the basis for reforms made during the administrations of Woodrow Wilson, Franklin D. Roosevelt, and other crusading Presidents. In short, even though the candidates of a third party have rarely won electoral votes, they have played an important role as gadflies and prophets. For that reason, any system that discourages the candidacies of the presidential nominees of third parties robs the American people of very useful critics.

## GREAT PRESIDENTS IN THE WHITE HOUSE

It is entirely possible that a highly qualified candidate may not become a great President. He is more likely to reach that rank, however, if he commands a well-organized, highly efficient executive department. From Woodrow Wilson onward, Presidents have complained that their burden is more than one man can bear—and yet each succeeding President has assumed more responsibility than his predecessors have had. Efforts to shift part of the load the President carries to other shoulders have resulted in the executive organization described in Chapter V. The present structure is the result of reorganizations that have been carried out by successive Presidents. The executive branch of government undoubtedly will be reorganized many times in the future, as each President attempts to make his administration effective. Sometimes a presidential candidate may make the reorganization of the executive branch a major issue, as Jimmy Carter did in 1976.

A reorganization of the executive branch is designed to

eliminate various agencies and to combine other divisions in the name of efficiency. President Nixon, for example, proposed to create a "super Cabinet" made up of a few key advisers who would oversee a great number of separate agencies. Instead of having to confer with many subordinates, President Nixon planned to consult with a few. The proposed reorganization was to concentrate decision making, and free the President to concentrate on major policy.

But it is easier to reorganize the executive department on paper than to carry the project out. Each executive department and agency has its friends in Congress and the country at large, so proposed changes ordinarily meet with stiff opposition. And efforts to streamline the executive branch are offset by the necessity of creating additional agencies to cope with national problems as they arise. The chart showing the present organization of the executive branch of government lists a number of agencies not found on similar charts drawn up only a few years ago.

A number of executive agencies have been established to deal with problems created by recent scientific discoveries and technological changes—such as television, atomic energy, ballistic missiles, and travel in outer space. Other agencies have been set up to advise the President regarding the vast socio-economic changes that have taken place in recent years—such as urbanization, mass education at the college level, and racial integration. The branch of government that the President heads has become more complicated in organization and more far-reaching in its influence for a very obvious reason. Almost from the beginning of the republic, the President has been the keystone of the American political system. Recently, he has become the keystone of the socio-economic structure as well. The people of the United States have a tendency to turn to the President for the solution of their every problem, and to expect him to protect them from disaster, foreign as well as domestic.

The demands that the American people make on their President result from the realization that life in what is supposedly the most secure country in the world is highly insecure. The air and the waters of the globe, once thought inexhaustible, have been found to be limited and in danger of destruction. The soil on which all life depends has been depleted, and many of the mineral resources that lie underneath it are already in short supply. Most Americans are aware that they cannot buy the products that their country produces so bountifully unless they have jobs—and unemployment is a specter that haunts millions of citizens. An American looking beyond the confines of his native land finds much that frightens him. He is less aware of the missiles that the United States has poised around the world to wipe out an enemy nation than he is to the dangers that enemy nations pose for him. When he dares to think of it, he realizes that hostile submarines constantly patrol the coasts of the United States, and that each of them carries enough warheads to destroy a large part of his country.

It is through this dangerous, uncertain world that the President of the United States is called to lead his people. Powerful as he is, there are many forces over which he has little or no control: unceasing technological change that transforms human life; the steady rise of the world's population and its shrinking resources; the growing demand of the hungry two thirds of the world to be fed, and of the nonwhite majority of the world to be free.

The demands now placed upon the President of the United States are far more crushing than those placed upon the "great" Presidents of the past. There is reason to believe that every future President must be great if this nation is to endure.

# APPENDICES

| NAME | BIRTHPLACE | DATE OF BIRTH | ANCESTRY | CHURCH AFFILIATION | EDUCATION |
|---|---|---|---|---|---|
| 1. GEORGE WASHINGTON | Wakefield, Westmoreland Co., Va. | Feb. 22, 1732 | English | Episcopalian | Limited education by tutors |
| 2. JOHN ADAMS | Quincy, Mass. | Oct. 30, 1735 | English | Unitarian | Graduated from Harvard University |
| 3. THOMAS JEFFERSON | Shadwell, Albemarle Co., Va. | Apr. 13, 1743 | Welsh | Practically a Unitarian but not a church member | Graduated from the College of William and Mary |
| 4. JAMES MADISON | Port Conway, King George Co., Va. | Mar. 16, 1751 | English | Episcopalian | Graduated from Princeton University |
| 5. JAMES MONROE | Westmoreland Co., Va. | Apr. 28, 1758 | Scotch-Welsh | Episcopalian | Attended the College of William and Mary |
| 6. JOHN QUINCY ADAMS | Quincy, Mass. | July 11, 1767 | English | Unitarian | Graduated from Harvard University |
| 7. ANDREW JACKSON | Waxhaw Settlement, border of N.C. and S.C. | Mar. 15, 1767 | Scotch-Irish | Presbyterian | Self-educated |
| 8. MARTIN VAN BUREN | Kinderhook, N.Y. | Dec. 5, 1782 | Dutch | Dutch Reformed | Attended public schools |
| 9. WILLIAM HENRY HARRISON | Berkeley, Charles City Co., Va. | Feb. 9, 1773 | English | Episcopalian | Attended Hampden-Sydney College |
| 10. JOHN TYLER | Greenway, Charles City Co., Va. | Mar. 29, 1790 | English | Episcopalian | Graduated from the College of William and Mary |
| 11. JAMES KNOX POLK | Mecklenburg Co., N.C. | Nov. 2, 1795 | Scotch-Irish | Methodist | Graduated from the University of North Carolina |
| 12. ZACHARY TAYLOR | Orange Co., Va. | Sept. 24, 1784 | English | Episcopalian | Self-educated |

# THE UNITED STATES

| OCCUPATION | RESIDENCE WHEN INAUGURATED | DATE OF INAUG. | AGE | POLITICAL PARTY | PLACE OF DEATH | DATE OF DEATH | BURIAL PLACE |
|---|---|---|---|---|---|---|---|
| Planter-soldier | Mount Vernon, Va. | 1789 | 57 | Federalist | Mount Vernon, Va. | Dec. 14, 1799 | Mount Vernon, Va. |
| Lawyer | Quincy, Mass. | 1797 | 61 | Federalist | Quincy, Mass. | July 4, 1826 | Quincy, Mass. |
| Planter-lawyer | Monticello, Va. | 1801 | 58 | Democratic Republican | Monticello, Va. | July 4, 1826 | Monticello, Va. |
| Planter | Montpelier, Orange Co., Va. | 1809 | 57 | Democratic Republican | Montpelier, Orange Co., Va. | June 28, 1836 | Montpelier, Orange Co., Va. |
| Planter-lawyer | Ash Lawn, Va. | 1817 | 58 | Democratic Republican | New York, N.Y. | July 4, 1831 | Richmond, Va. |
| Diplomat | Quincy, Mass. | 1825 | 57 | National Republican (Independent Federalist) | Washington, D.C. | Feb. 23, 1848 | Quincy, Mass. |
| Planter-lawyer-soldier | The Hermitage, Tenn. | 1829 | 61 | Democrat | The Hermitage, Tenn. | June 8, 1845 | The Hermitage, Tenn. |
| Lawyer | Kinderhook, N.Y. | 1837 | 54 | Democrat | Kinderhook, N.Y. | July 24, 1862 | Kinderhook, N.Y. |
| Soldier | North Bend, Ohio | 1841 | 68 | Whig | Washington, D.C. | Apr. 4, 1841 | North Bend, Ohio |
| Lawyer | Greenway, Charles City Co., Va. | 1841 | 51 | Whig | Richmond, Va. | Jan. 18, 1862 | Richmond, Va. |
| Lawyer | Nashville, Tenn. | 1845 | 49 | Democrat | Nashville, Tenn. | June 15, 1849 | Nashville, Tenn. |
| Planter-soldier | Baton Rouge, La. | 1849 | 64 | Whig | Washington, D.C. | July 9, 1850 | Louisville, Ky. |

| NAME | BIRTHPLACE | DATE OF BIRTH | ANCESTRY | CHURCH AFFILIATION | EDUCATION |
|---|---|---|---|---|---|
| 13.<br>MILLARD FILLMORE | Summerhill, Cayuga Co., N.Y. | Jan. 7, 1800 | English | Unitarian | Largely self-educated |
| 14.<br>FRANKLIN PIERCE | Hillsborough, N.H. | Nov. 23, 1804 | English | Episcopalian | Graduated from Bowdoin College |
| 15.<br>JAMES BUCHANAN | near Foltz, Franklin Co., Pa. | Apr. 23, 1791 | Scotch-Irish | Presbyterian | Graduated from Dickinson College |
| 16.<br>ABRAHAM LINCOLN | near Hodgenville, Ky. | Feb. 12, 1809 | English | None | Self-educated |
| 17.<br>ANDREW JOHNSON | Raleigh, N.C. | Dec. 29, 1808 | English | Methodist | Self-educated |
| 18.<br>ULYSSES SIMPSON GRANT | Point Pleasant, Ohio | Apr. 27, 1822 | English | None, but attended Methodist Church | Graduated from West Point |
| 19.<br>RUTHERFORD BIRCHARD HAYES | Delaware, Ohio | Oct. 4, 1822 | Scotch-Irish | Agnostic tendency, but attended Methodist Church | Graduate of Kenyon College and Harvard Law School |
| 20.<br>JAMES ABRAM GARFIELD | Orange, Cuyahoga Co., Ohio | Nov. 19, 1831 | English | Disciples of Christ | Attended Hiram College; graduated from Williams College |
| 21.<br>CHESTER ALAN ARTHUR | Fairfield, Franklin Co., Vt. | Oct. 5, 1830 | Scotch-Irish | Episcopalian | Graduated from Union College |
| 22.<br>(STEPHEN) GROVER CLEVELAND | Caldwell, N.J. | Mar. 18, 1837 | English | Presbyterian | Self-educated |
| 23.<br>BENJAMIN HARRISON | North Bend, Ohio | Aug. 20, 1833 | English | Presbyterian | Graduated from Miami University (Ohio) |

# THE UNITED STATES

| OCCUPATION | RESIDENCE WHEN INAUGURATED | DATE OF INAUG. | AGE | POLITICAL PARTY | PLACE OF DEATH | DATE OF DEATH | BURIAL PLACE |
|---|---|---|---|---|---|---|---|
| Teacher-lawyer | Buffalo, N.Y. | 1850 | 50 | Whig | Buffalo, N.Y. | Mar. 8, 1874 | Buffalo, N.Y. |
| Lawyer | Concord, N.H. | 1853 | 48 | Democrat | Concord, N.H. | Oct. 8, 1869 | Concord, N.H. |
| Lawyer | Wheatland, near Lancaster, Pa. | 1857 | 65 | Democrat | Wheatland near Lancaster, Pa. | June 1, 1868 | Wheatland, near Lancaster, Pa. |
| Lawyer | Springfield, Ill. | 1861 | 52 | Republican | Washington, D.C. | Apr. 14, 1865 | Springfield, Ill. |
| Tailor | Greenville, Tenn. | 1865 | 56 | Republican | Carter's Station, Tenn. | July 31, 1875 | Greenville, Tenn. |
| Soldier | Galena, Ill. | 1869 | 46 | Republican | New York, N.Y. | July 23, 1885 | New York, N.Y. |
| Lawyer | Cincinnati, Ohio | 1877 | 54 | Republican | Fremont, Ohio | Jan. 17, 1893 | Fremont, Ohio |
| Teacher | Mentor, Ohio | 1881 | 49 | Republican | Elberon, N.J. | Sept. 19, 1881 | Cleveland, Ohio |
| Teacher-lawyer | New York, N.Y. | 1881 | 50 | Republican | New York, N.Y. | Nov. 18, 1886 | Albany, N.Y. |
| Lawyer | Albany, N.Y. | 1885 | 47 | Democrat | Princeton, N.J. | June 24, 1908 | Princeton, N.J. |
| Lawyer | Indianapolis, Ind. | 1889 | 55 | Republican | Indianapolis, Ind. | Mar. 13, 1901 | Indianapolis, Ind. |

| NAME | BIRTHPLACE | DATE OF BIRTH | ANCESTRY | CHURCH AFFILIATION | EDUCATION |
|---|---|---|---|---|---|
| 24. GROVER CLEVELAND | Caldwell, N.J. | Mar. 18, 1837 | English | Presbyterian | Self-educated |
| 25. WILLIAM MC KINLEY | Niles, Trumbull Co., Ohio | Jan. 29, 1843 | Scotch-Irish | Methodist | Attended Allegheny College and Albany Law School |
| 26. THEODORE ROOSEVELT | New York, N.Y. | Oct. 27, 1858 | Dutch | Dutch Reformed | Graduated from Harvard University; attended Columbia Law School |
| 27. WILLIAM HOWARD TAFT | Cincinnati, Ohio | Sept. 15, 1857 | English | Unitarian | Graduated from Yale University and Cincinnati Law School |
| 28. WOODROW WILSON | Staunton, Va. | Dec. 28, 1856 | Scotch-Irish | Presbyterian | Attended Davidson College and the University of Virginia Law School; graduated from Princeton University and Johns Hopkins University |
| 29. WARREN GAMALIEL HARDING | Corsica, Morrow Co., Ohio | Nov. 2, 1865 | English | Baptist | Attended Ohio Central College |
| 30. CALVIN COOLIDGE | Plymouth, Vt. | July 4, 1872 | English | Congregationalist | Graduated from Amherst College |
| 31. HERBERT CLARK HOOVER | West Branch, Iowa | Aug. 10, 1874 | Swiss-German | Quaker | Graduated from Stanford University |
| 32. FRANKLIN DELANO ROOSEVELT | Hyde Park, Dutchess Co., N.Y. | Jan. 30, 1882 | Dutch | Episcopalian | Graduated from Harvard University; attended Columbia Law School |
| 33. HARRY S. TRUMAN | Lamar, Mo. | May 8, 1884 | Scotch-Irish-English | Baptist | Attended Independence, Missouri, public schools |

# THE UNITED STATES

| OCCUPATION | RESIDENCE WHEN INAUGURATED | DATE OF INAUG. | AGE | POLITICAL PARTY | PLACE OF DEATH | DATE OF DEATH | BURIAL PLACE |
|---|---|---|---|---|---|---|---|
| Lawyer | New York, N.Y. | 1893 | 55 | Democrat | Princeton, N.J. | June 24, 1908 | Princeton, N.J. |
| Lawyer | Canton, Ohio | 1897 | 54 | Republican | Buffalo, N.Y. | Sept. 14, 1901 | Canton, Ohio |
| Rancher-soldier | Albany, N.Y. | 1901 | 42 | Republican | Oyster Bay, L.I., N.Y. | Jan. 6, 1919 | Oyster Bay, L.I., N.Y. |
| Lawyer | Cincinnati, Ohio | 1909 | 51 | Republican | Washington, D.C. | Mar. 8, 1930 | Washington, D.C. |
| Teacher | Trenton, N.J. | 1913 | 56 | Democrat | Washington, D.C. | Feb. 3, 1924 | Washington, D.C. |
| Newspaper publisher | Marion, Ohio | 1921 | 55 | Republican | San Francisco, Calif. | Aug. 2, 1923 | Marion, Ohio |
| Lawyer | Northampton, Mass. | 1923 | 51 | Republican | Northampton, Mass. | Jan. 5, 1933 | Plymouth, Vt. |
| Engineer | Palo Alto, Calif. | 1929 | 54 | Republican | New York, N.Y. | Oct. 20, 1964 | West Branch, Iowa |
| Lawyer | Hyde Park, Dutchess Co., N.Y. | 1933 | 50 | Democrat | Warm Springs, Ga. | Apr. 12, 1945 | Hyde Park, Dutchess Co., N.Y. |
| Farmer-merchant | Independence, Mo. | 1945 | 60 | Democrat | Independence, Mo. | Dec. 26, 1972 | Independence, Mo. |

| NAME | BIRTHPLACE | DATE OF BIRTH | ANCESTRY | CHURCH AFFILIATION | EDUCATION |
|---|---|---|---|---|---|
| 34. DWIGHT DAVID EISENHOWER | Denison, Tex. | Oct. 14, 1890 | Swiss-German | Presbyterian | Graduated from West Point |
| 35. JOHN FITZGERALD KENNEDY | Brookline, Mass. | May 29, 1917 | Irish | Roman Catholic | Graduated from Harvard University |
| 36. LYNDON BAINES JOHNSON | Stonewall, Texas | Aug. 27, 1908 | English | Disciples of Christ | Graduated from S.W. Texas State Teachers College |
| 37. RICHARD MILHOUS NIXON | Yorba Linda, Calif. | Jan. 9, 1913 | English-Scotch-Irish | Quaker | Graduated from Whittier College, Duke Law School |
| 38. GERALD RUDOLF FORD | Omaha, Neb. | July 14, 1913 | English | Episcopalian | Graduated from Univ. Michigan, Yale Law School |
| 39. JIMMY CARTER | Plains, Ga. | Oct. 1, 1924 | English | Baptist | Graduated from U.S. Naval Academy |

# THE UNITED STATES

| OCCUPATION | RESIDENCE WHEN INAUGURATED | DATE OF INAUG. | AGE | POLITICAL PARTY | PLACE OF DEATH | DATE OF DEATH | BURIAL PLACE |
|---|---|---|---|---|---|---|---|
| Soldier | New York, N.Y. | 1953 | 62 | Republican | Washington, D.C. | March 28, 1969 | Abilene, Kansas |
| Journalist, Politician | Boston, Mass. | 1961 | 43 | Democrat | Dallas, Texas | Nov. 22, 1963 | Arlington, Va. |
| Teacher, Politician | Johnson City, Texas | 1963 | 55 | Democrat | Johnson City, Texas | Jan. 22, 1973 | Johnson City, Texas |
| Lawyer | New York, N.Y. | 1969 | 56 | Republican | | | |
| Lawyer | Grand Rapids, Michigan | 1974 | 61 | Republican | | | |
| Farmer-businessman | Plains, Ga. | 1977 | 52 | Democrat | | | |

# THE VICE-PRESIDENTS OF THE UNITED STATES

| NAME | BIRTHPLACE | BIRTH DATE | RESIDENCE WHEN QUALIFIED | YEAR | AGE | POLITICAL PARTY | PRESIDENT | PLACE OF DEATH | DATE OF DEATH |
|------|-----------|-----------|-------------------------|------|-----|-----------------|-----------|----------------|---------------|
| 1. JOHN ADAMS | Quincy, Mass. | Oct. 19, 1735 | Quincy, Mass. | 1789 | 53 | Federalist | George Washington | Quincy, Mass. | July 4, 1826 |
| 2. THOMAS JEFFERSON | Shadwell, Va. | Apr. 13, 1743 | Monticello, Va. | 1797 | 53 | Federalist | John Adams | Monticello, Va. | July 4, 1826 |
| 3. AARON BURR | Newark, N.J. | Feb. 6, 1756 | New York, N.Y. | 1801 | 44 | Democratic Republican | Thomas Jefferson | Staten Island, N.Y. | Sept. 14, 1836 |
| 4. GEORGE CLINTON | Little Britain, N.Y. | July 26, 1739 | Albany, N.Y. | 1805 | 65 | Democratic Republican | Thomas Jefferson | Washington, D.C. | Apr. 20, 1812 |
| 5. ELBRIDGE GERRY | Marblehead, Mass. | July 17, 1744 | Boston, Mass. | 1813 | 68 | Democratic Republican | James Madison | Washington, D.C. | Nov. 23, 1814 |
| 6. DANIEL D. TOMPKINS | Scarsdale, N.Y. | June 21, 1774 | Albany, N.Y. | 1817 | 42 | Democratic Republican | James Monroe | Staten Island, N.Y. | June 11, 1825 |
| 7. JOHN CALDWELL CALHOUN | Abbeville, S.C. | Mar. 18, 1782 | Abbeville, S.C. | 1825 | 42 | National Republican (Independent Federalist) | John Quincy Adams | Washington, D.C. | Mar. 31, 1850 |

| # | Name | Birthplace | Birthdate | | Year | Age | Party | President | Death place | Death date |
|---|------|-----------|-----------|---|------|-----|-------|-----------|-----------|-----------|
| 8. | MARTIN VAN BUREN | Kinderhook, N.Y. | Dec. 5, 1782 | Kinderhook, N.Y. | 1838 | 50 | Democrat | Andrew Jackson | Kinderhook, N.Y. | July 24, 1862 |
| 9. | RICHARD MENTOR JOHNSON | Floyd's Station, near Louisville, Ky. | Oct. 17, 1780 | Frankfort, Ky. | 1837 | 56 | Democrat | Martin Van Buren | Frankfort, Ky. | Nov. 19, 1850 |
| 10. | JOHN TYLER | Greenway, Va. | Mar. 29, 1790 | Greenway, Va. | 1841 | 50 | Whig | William Henry Harrison | Richmond, Va. | Jan. 18, 1862 |
| 11. | GEORGE MIFFLIN DALLAS | Philadelphia, Pa. | July 10, 1792 | Philadelphia, Pa. | 1845 | 52 | Democrat | James Knox Polk | Philadelphia, Pa. | Dec. 31, 1864 |
| 12. | MILLARD FILLMORE | Summerhill, N.Y. | Jan. 7, 1800 | Buffalo, N.Y. | 1849 | 49 | Whig | Zachary Taylor | Buffalo, N.Y. | Mar. 8, 1874 |
| 13. | WILLIAM RUFUS DEVANE KING | Sampson, Co., N.C. | Apr. 6, 1786 | near Cahawba, Dallas Co., Ala. | 1853 | 66 | Democrat | Franklin Pierce | near Cahawba, Dallas Co., Ala. | Apr. 17, 1853 |
| 14. | JOHN CABELL BRECKENRIDGE | near Lexington, Ky. | Jan. 21, 1821 | Lexington, Ky. | 1857 | 36 | Democrat | James Buchanan | Lexington, Ky. | May 17, 1875 |
| 15. | HANNIBAL HAMLIN | Paris Hill, Maine | Aug. 27, 1809 | Paris, Maine | 1861 | 51 | Republican | Abraham Lincoln | Bangor, Maine | July 4, 1891 |

# THE VICE-PRESIDENTS OF THE UNITED STATES

| NAME | BIRTHPLACE | BIRTH DATE | RESIDENCE WHEN QUALIFIED | YEAR | AGE | POLITICAL PARTY | PRESIDENT | PLACE OF DEATH | DATE OF DEATH |
|---|---|---|---|---|---|---|---|---|---|
| 16. ANDREW JOHNSON | Raleigh, N.C. | Dec. 29, 1808 | Greenville, Tenn. | 1865 | 56 | Republican | Abraham Lincoln | Carter's Station, Carter Co., Tenn. | July 30, 1875 |
| 17. SCHUYLER COLFAX | New York, N.Y. | Mar. 23, 1823 | South Bend, Ind. | 1869 | 45 | Republican | Ulysses Simpson Grant | Mankato, Minn. | Jan. 13, 1885 |
| 18. HENRY WILSON | Farmington, N.H. | Feb. 16, 1812 | Natick, Mass. | 1873 | 61 | Republican | Ulysses Simpson Grant | Washington, D.C. | Nov. 22, 1875 |
| 19. WILLIAM ALMON WHEELER | Malone, N.Y. | June 30, 1819 | Malone, N.Y. | 1877 | 57 | Republican | Rutherford Birchard Hayes | Malone, N.Y. | June 4, 1887 |
| 20. CHESTER ALAN ARTHUR | Fairfield, Vt. | Oct. 5, 1830 | New York, N.Y. | 1881 | 50 | Republican | James Abram Garfield | New York, N.Y. | Nov. 18, 1886 |
| 21. THOMAS ANDREWS HENDRICKS | near Zanesville, Muskingum Co., Ohio | Sept. 7, 1819 | Indianapolis, Ind. | 1885 | 65 | Democrat | Grover Cleveland | Indianapolis, Ind. | Nov. 25, 1885 |

| No. / Name | Birthplace | Birth date | | Year | Age | Party | President | | Death date |
|---|---|---|---|---|---|---|---|---|---|
| 22. LEVI PARSONS MORTON | Shoreham, Vt. | May 16, 1824 | New York, N.Y. | 1889 | 64 | Republican | Benjamin Harrison | Rhinebeck, N.Y. | May 16, 1920 |
| 23. ADLAI EWING STEVENSON | Christian Co., Ky. | Oct. 23, 1835 | Metamora, Ill. | 1893 | 57 | Democrat | Grover Cleveland | Chicago, Ill. | June 13, 1914 |
| 24. GARRETT AUGUSTUS HOBART | Long Branch, N.J. | June 3, 1844 | Paterson, N.J. | 1897 | 52 | Republican | William McKinley | Paterson, N.J. | Nov. 21, 1899 |
| 25. THEODORE ROOSEVELT | New York, N.Y. | Oct. 27, 1858 | Albany, N.Y. | 1901 | 42 | Republican | William McKinley | Oyster Bay, L.I., N.Y. | Jan. 6, 1919 |
| 26. CHARLES WARREN FAIRBANKS | Unionville Center, Ohio | May 11, 1852 | Indianapolis, Ind. | 1905 | 52 | Republican | Theodore Roosevelt | Indianapolis, Ind. | June 4, 1918 |
| 27. JAMES SCHOOLCRAFT SHERMAN | near Utica, N.Y. | Oct. 24, 1855 | Utica, N.Y. | 1909 | 53 | Republican | William Howard Taft | Utica, N.Y. | Oct. 30, 1912 |
| 28. THOMAS R. MARSHALL | North Manchester, Ind. | Mar. 14, 1854 | Indianapolis, Ind. | 1913 | 58 | Democrat | Woodrow Wilson | Washington, D.C. | June 1, 1925 |
| 29. CALVIN COOLIDGE | Plymouth, Vt. | July 4, 1872 | Northampton, Mass. | 1921 | 48 | Republican | Warren Gamaliel Harding | Northampton, Mass. | Jan. 5, 1933 |

# THE VICE-PRESIDENTS OF THE UNITED STATES

| NAME | BIRTHPLACE | BIRTH DATE | RESIDENCE WHEN QUALIFIED | YEAR | AGE | POLITICAL PARTY | PRESIDENT | PLACE OF DEATH | DATE OF DEATH |
|---|---|---|---|---|---|---|---|---|---|
| 30. CHARLES GATES DAWES | Marietta, Ohio | Aug. 27, 1865 | Evanston, Ill. | 1925 | 59 | Republican | Calvin Coolidge | Evanston, Ill. | Apr. 23, 1951 |
| 31. CHARLES CURTIS | North Topeka, Kans. | Jan. 25, 1860 | Topeka, Kan. | 1929 | 68 | Republican | Herbert Clark Hoover | Washington, D.C. | Feb. 8, 1936 |
| 32. JOHN NANCE GARNER | Red River Co., Tex. | Nov. 22, 1869 | Clarksville, Tex. | 1933 | 63 | Democrat | Franklin Delano Roosevelt | Uvalde, Tex. | Nov. 7, 1967 |
| 33. HENRY AGARD WALLACE | Adair Co., Iowa | Oct. 7, 1888 | Adair Co., Iowa | 1941 | 52 | Democrat | Franklin Delano Roosevelt | Danbury, Conn. | Nov. 18, 1965 |
| 34. HARRY S. TRUMAN | Lamar, Mo. | May 8, 1884 | Independence, Mo. | 1945 | 60 | Democrat | Franklin Delano Roosevelt | Independence, Mo. | Dec. 26, 1972 |
| 35. ALBEN WILLIAM BARKLEY | Graves Co., Ky. | Nov. 24, 1877 | Paducah, McCracken Co., Ky. | 1949 | 71 | Democrat | Harry S. Truman | Lexington, Va. | April 30, 1956 |
| 36. RICHARD MILHOUS NIXON | Yorba Linda, Calif. | Jan. 9, 1913 | Whittier, Calif. | 1953 | 40 | Republican | Dwight David Eisenhower | | |

| | | | | | | | | | |
|---|---|---|---|---|---|---|---|---|---|
| 37. LYNDON B. JOHNSON | Stonewall, Texas | Aug. 27, 1908 | Johnson City, Tex. | 1963 | 55 | Democrat | John F. Kennedy | Johnson City, Tex. | Jan. 22, 1973 |
| 38. HUBERT H. HUMPHREY | Wallace, S.D. | May 27, 1911 | Minneapolis, Minn. | 1965 | 54 | Democrat | Lyndon B. Johnson | | |
| 39. SPIRO AGNEW | Baltimore, Md. | Nov. 9, 1918 | Baltimore, Md. | 1969 | 51 | Republican | Richard Milhous Nixon | | |
| 40. GERALD R. FORD | Omaha, Neb. | July 14, 1913 | Grand Rapids, Mich. | 1973 | 60 | Republican | Richard Milhous Nixon | | |
| 41. NELSON A. ROCKEFELLER | Bar Harbor, Me. | July 8, 1908 | New York, N.Y. | 1974 | 66 | Republican | Gerald R. Ford | | |
| 42. WALTER F. MONDALE | Ceylon, Minn. | Jan. 5, 1928 | Afton, Minn. | 1977 | 49 | Democrat | Jimmy Carter | | |

# THE CONSTITUTION OF THE UNITED STATES

(Articles relating principally to the Presidency)

## ARTICLE II

*Section 1.* (1) The Executive power shall be vested in a President of the United States of America. He shall hold his office during the term of four years, and, together with the Vice-President, chosen for the same term, be elected, as follows:

(2) Each State shall appoint, in such manner as the Legislature thereof may direct, a number of electors, equal to the whole number of Senators and Representatives to which the State may be entitled in the Congress: but no Senator or Representative, or person holding an office of trust or profit under the United States, shall be appointed an elector.

[The electors shall meet in their respective States, and vote by ballot for two persons, of whom one at least shall not be an inhabitant of the same State with themselves. And they shall make a list of all the persons voted for, and of the number of votes for each; which list they shall sign and certify, and transmit sealed to the seat of the government of the United States, directed to the President of the Senate. The President of the Senate shall, in the presence of the Senate and House of Representatives, open all the certificates, and the votes shall then be counted. The person having the greatest number of votes shall be the President, if such number be a majority of the whole number of electors appointed; and if there be more than one who have such majority, and have an equal number of votes, then the House of Representatives shall immediately choose by ballot one of them for President; and if no person have a majority, then from the five highest on the list the said House shall in like manner choose the President. But in choosing the President, the votes shall be taken by States, the representation from each State having one vote; a quorum for this purpose shall consist of a member or members from two-thirds of the States, and a majority of all the States shall be necessary to a choice. In every case, after the choice of the President, the person having the greatest number of votes of the electors shall be the Vice-President. But if there should remain two or more who have equal votes, the Senate shall choose from them by ballot the Vice-President.][1]

(3) The Congress may determine the time of choosing the electors, and the day on which they shall give their votes; which day shall be the same throughout the United States.

(4) No person except a natural-born citizen, or a citizen of the United States, at the time of the adoption of this Constitution, shall be eligible to the office of President; neither shall any person be eligible to that office who shall not have attained to the age of thirty-five years, and been fourteen years a resident within the United States.

(5) In case of the removal of the President from office, or of his death,

---

1 This paragraph superseded by Amendment XII, which has, in turn, been modified by Amendment XX.

resignation, or inability to discharge the powers and duties of the said office, the same shall devolve on the Vice-President, and the Congress may by law provide for the case of removal, death, resignation, or inability, both of the President and Vice-President, declaring what officer shall then act as President, and such officer shall act accordingly, until the disability be removed, or a President shall be elected.

(6) The President shall, at stated times, receive for his services a compensation, which shall neither be increased nor diminished during the period for which he shall have been elected, and he shall not receive within that period any other emolument from the United States, or any of them.

(7) Before he enter on the execution of his office, he shall take the following oath or affirmation: "I do solemnly swear (or affirm) that I will faithfully execute the office of President of the United States, and will, to the best of my ability, preserve, protect, and defend the Constitution of the United States."

Section 2. (1) The President shall be commander in chief of the army and navy of the United States, and of the militia of the several States, when called into the actual service of the United States; he may require the opinion, in writing, of the principal officer in each of the executive departments, upon any subject relating to the duties of their respective offices, and he shall have power to grant reprieves and pardons for offenses against the United States, except in cases of impeachment.

(2) He shall have power, by and with the advice and consent of the Senate, to make treaties, provided two-thirds of the Senators present concur; and he shall nominate, and by and with the advice and consent of the Senate, shall appoint ambassadors, other public ministers and consuls, judges of the Supreme Court, and all other officers of the United States, whose appointments are not herein otherwise provided for, and which shall be established by law: but the Congress may by law vest the appointment of such inferior officers, as they think proper, in the President alone, in the courts of law, or in the heads of departments.

(3) The President shall have power to fill up all vacancies that may happen during the recess of the Senate, by granting commissions which shall expire at the end of their next session.

Section 3. He shall from time to time give to the Congress information of the state of the Union, and recommend to their consideration such measures as he shall judge necessary and expedient; he may, on extraordinary occasions, convene both Houses, or either of them, and in case of disagreement between them, with respect to the time of adjournment, he may adjourn them to such time as he shall think proper; he shall receive ambassadors and other public ministers; he shall take care that the laws be faithfully executed, and shall commission all the officers of the United States.

Section 4. The President, Vice-President, and all civil officers of the United States, shall be removed from office on impeachment for, and conviction of, treason, bribery, or other high crimes and misdemeanors.

## AMENDMENT XII[2]

The electors shall meet in their respective States, and vote by ballot for President and Vice-President, one of whom, at least, shall not be an

2 Proclaimed September 25, 1804.

THE CONSTITUTION OF THE UNITED STATES

inhabitant of the same State with themselves; they shall name in their ballots the person voted for as President, and in distinct ballots the person voted for as Vice-President, and they shall make distinct lists of all persons voted for as President, and of all persons voted for as Vice-President, and of the number of votes for each, which lists they shall sign and certify, and transmit sealed to the seat of the Government of the United States, directed to the President of the Senate;—the President of the Senate shall, in the presence of the Senate and House of Representatives, open all the certificates, and the votes shall then be counted;—The person having the greatest number of votes for President, shall be the President, if such number be a majority of the whole number of Electors appointed; and if no person have such majority, then from the persons having the highest numbers not exceeding three on the list of those voted for as President, the House of Representatives shall choose immediately, by ballot, the President. But in choosing the President, the votes shall be taken by States, the representation from each State having one vote; a quorum for this purpose shall consist of a member or members from two-thirds of the States, and a majority of all the States shall be necessary to a choice. And if the House of Representatives shall not choose a President whenever the right of choice shall devolve upon them, before the fourth day of March next following, then the Vice-President shall act as President, as in the case of the death or other constitutional disability of the President. The person having the greatest number of votes as Vice-President, shall be the Vice-President, if such number be a majority of the whole number of Electors appointed, and if no person have a majority, then from the two highest numbers on the list, the Senate shall choose the Vice-President; a quorum for the purpose shall consist of two-thirds of the whole number of Senators, and a majority of the whole number shall be necessary to a choice. But no person constitutionally ineligible to the office of President shall be eligible to that of Vice-President of the United States.

## AMENDMENT XX[3]

*Section 1.* The terms of the President and Vice-President shall end at noon on the 20th day of January, and the terms of Senators and Representatives at noon on the 3rd day of January, of the years in which such terms would have ended if this article had not been ratified; and the terms of their successors shall then begin.

*Section 2.* The Congress shall assemble at least once in every year, and such meeting shall begin at noon on the 3rd day of January, unless they shall by law appoint a different day.

*Section 3.* If, at the time fixed for the beginning of the term of the President, the President elect shall have died, the Vice-President elect shall become President. If a President shall not have been chosen before the time fixed for the beginning of his term, or if the President elect shall have failed to qualify, then the Vice-President elect shall act as President until a President shall have qualified; and the Congress may by law provide for the case wherein neither a President elect nor a Vice-President elect shall have qualified, declaring who shall then act as President, or the manner in which

3 Proclaimed February 6, 1933.

one who is to act shall be selected, and such person shall act accordingly until a President or Vice-President shall have qualified.

*Section 4.* The Congress may by law provide for the case of the death of any of the persons from whom the House of Representatives may choose a President whenever the right of choice shall have devolved upon them, and for the case of the death of any of the persons from whom the Senate may choose a Vice-President whenever the right of choice shall have devolved upon them.

*Section 5.* Sections 1 and 2 shall take effect on the 15th day of October following the ratification of this article.

*Section 6.* This article shall be inoperative unless it shall have been ratified as an amendment to the Constitution by the legislatures of three-fourths of the several States within seven years from the date of its submission.

## AMENDMENT XXII[4]

*Section 1.* No person shall be elected to the office of the President more than twice, and no person who has held the office of President, or acted as President, for more than two years of a term to which some other person was elected President shall be elected to the office of the President more than once. But this Article shall not apply to any person holding the office of President when this Article was proposed by the Congress, and shall not prevent any person who may be holding the office of President, or acting as President, during the term within which this Article becomes operative from holding the office of President, or acting as President during the remainder of such term.

*Section 2.* This Article shall be inoperative unless it shall have been ratified as an amendment to the Constitution by the legislatures of three-fourths of the several States within seven years from the date of its submission to the States by the Congress.

## AMENDMENT XXIII

*Section 1.* The District constituting the seat of Government of the United States shall appoint in such manner as the Congress may direct:

A number of electors of President and Vice-President equal to the whole number of Senators and Representatives in Congress to which the District would be entitled if it were a State, but in no event more than the least populous State; they shall be in addition to those appointed by the States, but they shall be considered, for the purposes of the election of President and Vice-President, to be electors appointed by a State; and they shall meet in the District and perform such duties as provided by the twelfth article of amendment.

*Section 2.* The Congress shall have power to enforce this article by appropriate legislation.[5]

## AMENDMENT XXIV

*Section 1.* The right of citizens of the United States to vote in any primary or other election for President or Vice-President, or for Senators or Representatives in Congress, shall not be denied or abridged by the

4 Adopted February 27, 1951.
5 Adopted March 29, 1961.

United States or any State by reason of failure to pay any poll tax or other tax.

Section 2. The Congress shall have power to enforce this article by appropriate legislation.[6]

## AMENDMENT XXV

Section 1. In case of the removal of the President from office or his death or resignation, the Vice-President shall become President.

Section 2. Whenever there is a vacancy in the office of the Vice-President, the President shall nominate a Vice-President who shall take the office upon confirmation by a majority vote of both houses of Congress.

Section 3. Whenever the President transmits to the President pro tempore of the Senate and the Speaker of the House of Representatives his written declaration that he is unable to discharge the powers and duties of his office, and until he transmits to them a written declaration to the contrary, such powers and duties shall be discharged by the Vice-President as Acting President.

Section 4. Whenever the Vice-President and a majority of either the principal officers of the executive department or of such other body as Congress may by law provide, transmit to the President pro tempore of the Senate and the Speaker of the House of Representatives their written declaration that the President is unable to discharge the powers and duties of his office, the Vice-President shall immediately assume the powers and duties of the office as Acting President.

Thereafter, when the President transmits to the President pro tempore of the Senate and the Speaker of the House of Representatives his written declaration that no inability exists, he shall resume the powers and duties of his office unless the Vice-President and a majority of either the principal officers of the executive department or of such other body as Congress may by law provide, transmit within four days to the President pro tempore of the Senate and the Speaker of the House of Representatives their written declaration that the President is unable to discharge the powers and duties of his office. Thereupon Congress shall decide the issue, assembling within 48 hours for that purpose if not in session. If the Congress, within 21 days after receipt of the latter written declaration, or, if Congress is not in session, within 21 days after Congress is required to assemble, determines by two-thirds vote of both houses that the President is unable to discharge the powers and duties of his office, the Vice-President shall continue to discharge the same as Acting President; otherwise, the President shall resume the powers and duties of his office.[7]

## AMENDMENT XXVI

Section 1. The right of citizens of the United States, who are eighteen years of age or older, to vote shall not be denied or abridged by the United States or any state on account of age.

Section 2. The Congress shall have the power to enforce this article by appropriate legislation.[8]

6 Adopted January 23, 1964.
7 Adopted February 10, 1967.
8 Adopted July 5, 1971.

# SUGGESTED READING

## REFERENCES

Diamond, Robert A. *Presidential Elections Since 1789*. Washington, D.C.: Congressional Quarterly, Inc., 1975.

Polsby, Nelson, and Aaron Wildavsky. *Presidential Elections*. New York: Charles Scribner's Sons, 1976.

Taylor, Tim. *The Book of Presidents*. New York: Arno Press, 1972.

United States Office of the Federal Register, National Archives and Records Service. *United States Government Manual*. Washington, D.C.: U.S. Government Printing Office, Annual.

## PICTORIAL HISTORIES

Cunliffe, Marcus. *The American Heritage History of the Presidency*. New York: American Heritage Publishing Co., Inc., 1968.

Lorant, Stefan. *The Glorious Burden*. New York: Harper & Row, Publishers, 1968.

## STUDIES OF THE PRESIDENCY

Barber, James D. *The Presidential Character*. Englewood Cliffs, N.J.: Prentice-Hall, Inc., 1972.

Hughes, Emmet John. *The Living Presidency*. Baltimore: Penguin Books, Inc., 1974.

Koenig, Louis W. *The Chief Executive*. New York: Harcourt, Brace & World, Inc., 1968.

Neustadt, Richard E. *Presidential Power: The Politics of Leadership*. New York: John Wiley & Sons, Inc., 1976.

Reedy, George E. *The Twilight of the Presidency*. Cleveland: The World Publishing Company, 1970.

Russell, Francis. *The President Makers*. Boston: Little, Brown and Company, 1976.

Schell, Jonathan. *The Time of Illusion*. New York: Alfred A. Knopf, 1976.

Schlesinger, Arthur M., Jr., *The Imperial Presidency*. Boston: Houghton Mifflin Company, 1973.

White, Theodore H. *The Making of the President 1960*. New York: Atheneum Publishers, 1962.

## STUDIES OF THE VICE-PRESIDENCY

Cohen, Richard M. and Jules Witcover. *A Heartbeat Away*. New York: The Viking Press, Inc., 1974.

Di Salle, Michael V., with Lawrence G. Blochman. *Second Choice: The Story of the United States Vice-Presidency*. New York: Hawthorn Books, Inc., 1966.

# INDEX

## ABOUT THE AUTHOR

Ernest B. Fincher was born in New Mexico. He received a B.A. degree from Texas Technological University, an M.A. degree from Columbia University, and a Ph.D. degree from New York University; and he is now professor emeritus of political science at the New Jersey State College at Montclair. He is a member of the American Academy of Political and Social Science.

Dr. Fincher is the author of six other books, including *The Government of the United States, In a Race with Time,* and *Spanish Americans As a Political Factor in New Mexico.* When he is not writing, he enjoys working on his New Jersey farm.